From I Am
To I Am,
With Love

A Guide To The End of Your
Personal Psychological Suffering

In The Timeless Being That You Actually Are,
There IS No Suffering. Discover How You Can
Realize This Yourself, Using The Pointers In
This Book: Right Here Right Now.

Charlie Hayes

The Image on the cover is a rendition
of the Japanese "Kanji" for Love.

(Cover Photo © Martin Pfetscher.
Image from BigStockPhoto.com.)

To order additional copies, please contact us.
BookSurge, LLC
www.booksurge.com
1-866-308-6235
orders@booksurge.com

Preface

This work is dedicated to "Sailor" Bob Adamson and the Ancient and Sacred Lineage of great beings known as the *Navnath Sampradaya*. In recent times, the expression of this Lineage came out through the Indian Sage, Sri Nisargadatta Maharaj.

My Teacher Bob Adamson's search for the Real ended in the presence of Nisargadatta in the late seventies. Since then Bob has shared this knowedge of The Natural State of true peace with many seekers around the globe. I am privileged to call Bob not only my Teacher, but also my Friend.

Lineage: The Navnath Sampradaya

The Sanskrit word *Nath* is the proper name of a *siddha sampradaya* (initiatory tradition) and the word itself literally means Lord, Protector, or Refuge. The related Sanskrit term *Adi Nath* means first or original Lord and is therefore a synonym for Shiva, Mahadeva, or Maheshvara and beyond these mental concepts, the Supreme Absolute Reality as the originator of all things.

The *Navnath Sampradaya*, a development of the earlier *Siddha* or *Avadhut Sampradaya*, is an ancient lineage of spiritual masters. Its founding is traditionally ascribed to Shri Bhagavan Dattatreya, considered by some to have been an incarnation of Lord Shiva.

The Publisher

I am grateful to Burt Jurgens for taking on the task of bringing the message of authentic non-duality out. The "spiritual world" is rife with misconceptions, one-sided teachings and other nonsense that often makes the suffering of a sincere seeker of truth worse.

Burt's publishing house expresses a profound commitment to cutting through the noise and smoke of these false teachings, thereby exposing the myths and foolish interpretations of the true Sage's pointers to what is real and what is not. His efforts are much needed and most welcome.

Acknowledgments

To my parents, Charles David and Barbara Hight Hayes, with the greatest love and devotion. They both showed me what real and honest courage looks like.

To my sons Charles David Hayes III and Charles Edward Hayes, who turned out very well indeed, in spite of my goofy life story. Charles kept showing me that I had something to live for when the suffering was at its worst... him, and his bride Rachel and my granddaughter Sarah. More love than words can ever capture.

A special thank you goes to my best buddy Werner Erhard, who taught me early on that until we know our Self as Being, Empty and Meaningless, nothing is directly known, because all our knowing is skewed toward some outcome in time... and time itself is a concept, not actually real in The Eternal Is that we are.

That it took so much "time" for the "penny to drop" was through no fault of Werner's. It was all about me, until the me disappeared in the Is of the Natural Eternal State of Simply Being.

There are others, all of whom helped in their own inimitable way:

Among them I count The Maharishi Mahesh Yogi, Swami Muktananda, Swamis Nityananda and Chidvilasananda, Dr. Fernando Flores, Dr. David Sodaro, His Holiness Sri Sri Ravi Shankar, Wayne Liquorman, Tony Parsons, Leo Hartong, Kali Ishaya, and Nathan Gill.

"Final Teachers"

Ultimately I owe the freedom from all suffering to the Oneness ItSelf, appearing as the following wonderful friends:

"Sailor" Bob Adamson,
and his "graduates:"

John Wheeler,
Gilbert Schultz,
Stephen Wingate,
John Greven,
Burt Jurgens,
and Annette Nibley

All Are I Am... as are You.
Not Many, Not Two, Not One

Contact the Author

Your comments, questions,
insights are most welcome...
e-mail: charliehayes36@yahoo.com
phone: USA 1-714-708-2311

Foreword: The Amazing Journey
Coming Back to Timeless Being...
The Home We Never Left.

The journey of Self discovery is the most wonderful, frightening, and exciting journey in this dream of life and living!

This is a book for seekers. If you have been on a spiritual quest, whether for 30 years or 30 days, this book is designed as a communication from your True Nature direct to That which knows that you ARE what you seek: That simple "I Am," that you are in truth, That which is universal and unbounded.

There is a radical and revolutionary message contained in the words and spaces of this book, AND there is an Energy-Intelligence that is at the heart of the message... a silent throb of pure consciousness that communicates outside of time and space. That Consciousness... Timeless Being... has been hiding in plain sight... right before your very eyes. This book, when read with trust and openness, can reveal that which is Always So as your authentic True Nature... directly, here and now.

To know the always so is to be illumined.

*−*Lao Tzu

There is nothing missing in what you truly are. You need not change, or evolve, or purify, to BE what you already are. In fact, all such attempts to "get to" what you are will naturally fail. Because you already ARE what you are... perfect, stainless, being-awareness, self-shining and ever-fresh!

There is only Wholeness, Unicity, Beingness... arising as an impersonal knowing that what you are has never been lacking in any way. The essence of Life that is at the heart of all matter, the simple knowingness that "Non-Conceptual, Impersonal Existence Is, and I Am That", is absolutely undeniable... and inexpressible. *The words only point to That which cannot be known by the mind.*

Right NOW you ALREADY ARE Your True Nature. What were the ancients and the sages referring to as our REAL Self?

It is Just This:

You exist and you are aware. What you sought and needed to know was only ever this.

You are this Non-Dual Presence Awareness... simply Being. The direct knowing of this Being is the living AS an incomprehensible Peace that surpasses understanding.

Full stop.

Around now, you might ask, "OK, but what about suffering? I have heard some teachers say that suffering is Oneness and nothing can be done about it because there is no person therefore suffering must endure."

The idea that suffering is inevitable comes out of the notion that who we are is totally powerless. But in actual fact what we truly are is ALL power, ALL knowingness, ALL Presence. Omnipotence, Omnipresence, Omniscience. That Source of ALL life and the entire manifestation is what we REALLY are... and one of the worst things the mind does is limit that with words!

What a Paradox!

This is the grand paradox: There is NO such thing as a separate person in the organism apart from this Omnipotence, Omniscience and Omnipresence. AND the innate intelligence-energy that keeps the stars in perfect order can certainly come to bear on human suffering. Now hear this: Suffering Is Optional! Keep it if you like, but if you are interested in living free of that unnecessary evil keep reading and looking within, with your OWN natural intelligence (NOT the mind, the answer is not in your thinking mind!)

By the way what to do with a paradox? Don't try to resolve it... that will make the mind crazy. Sit with it like a brick in your lap. Just BE with it.

Here is a central pointer toward the end of suffering: ALL suffering is based on the idea of a separate "me"... a person in the machine. But is there any such thing? Apart from a thought of an "I" is there any actual entity anywhere in there?

For "me," looking, looking like my life depended on it (because it did!) was the key. I absolutely cannot find a "me" or an "I" or a "myself"... it is absent.

But this cannot be accepted or believed. IT HAS TO BE SEEN through a no holds barred investigation. Do or die.

In this Presence Awareness, there is NO suffering.

This is The Home you never left.

Now, again there is a huge paradox in all this. In truth there is no person. It is not that there is nothing to be done; it is that there IS no one to do or not do anything. But so long as we do not live in and as that Understanding, then looking needs to happen. It is sort of like this: So long as you think you are the "doer" of actions, take the actions of looking within, doing the inquiry. What do you have to lose? Your suffering.

So, there is no one; AND so long as it seems there is someone, there is suffering, and the investigation needs to happen. THEN, once the gateless gate has been passed, then it is seen, by no one, that there never was a separate character. Now, Life flows simply and effortlessly... for no one. As it always did, as is Realized.

All is just happening in this that you are... Awareness-Presence.

So both the search... and the suffering... DO end. But NOT because someone finds something. It is simply seen that there is nothing to find, and no one to find it. You already are That which is sought.

Nothing in This Book Is "The Truth."

As we go on we will delve into these points in a variety of ways. Rather than try to figure out what is right or wrong about what's being said; look onto the space of your own natural awareness, and see what you see. What you discover might just surprise... and delight... you.

To paraphrase the sage Sri Nisargadatta Maharaj, once you realize, no kidding, that nothing can trouble you but your own imagination, you are free in and as your self-shining, unbounded, True Nature.

What does that mean? Simply this: All words are concepts, language, letters — at bottom just sounds. Is the sound in your ears of "water" ever going to quench your thirst?

8

No. The word water, no matter how loudly or lovingly said, will never BE water. The word water is a representation of a substance known to be clear, wet, and thirst-quenching.

Similarly, the concepts in this book represent certain "spaces" which cannot be captured by concepts or sounds or pictures... because the SPACE is BEYOND all such forms and formulations.

So look where the concepts point, never taking the concept to be the Real.

The truth cannot be captured by words and images.

The Tao that can be told is NOT the Eternal Tao.
—Lao Tzu

What does that mean?
Who asks that question??

Table of Contents

Part 1: The Pointers

Part 2: The Dialogues

Introduction: "The Natural State of Man Is JOY"

I saw this quote at my doctor's office in 1974. I was a very long way from Joy, but it became a sort of "naked possibility" for me.

If you suspend the skepticism and cynicism and look in the way the pointers in this book offer, those pointers, and the sharing of various seekers in dialogue in Part Two will naturally awaken your True Stateless State of Absolute Freedom and Natural Joy.

The Good News is that this Natural State has never actually been missing! Find out for yourself... and return to Timeless Being – The Home you Never Left.

As this nameless, timeless essence unfolds, that natural state of Joy is seen not as a thing to get someday. It is who I am. Who YOU Are. Who every one is.

Tired Of Suffering?

This is a book for those who are fed up with "spiritual seeking" and "psychological suffering" - *depression, anxiety, insecurity, fearfulness, anger* – all of which make life miserable for those afflicted by these things. I know. I suffered from depression and bipolar disorder for 64 years. (Yes, 64 years, from the age of five.) I was often suicidal, and medications didn't work. For a long time, I prayed to die.

While I feel the story of "me" is of no real value in the grand scheme of things — not that there actually IS a "grand scheme of things"! — some who still believe they are a suffering phantom character may find it useful... just understand, I AM NOT THE STORY. The best way to describe ANY "story of a person" would be with the words of Shakespeare: it is "a tale told by an idiot, filled with sound and fury, signifying... nothing."

My story is not all that unique, in its essence of swings from pleasure to pain and back again, over and over until it finally prompted investigation into what the real was - spirituality or "God" perhaps — and what the unreal also was — ego maybe?

Perhaps in essence my story is similar to your own. If you see yourself in what I share here, there may be an opening into a new space to be... just be, without a story. Is it possible to live as a space of freedom, power and love without being a separate entity scared to death it won't survive? Or worse that it will survive in some horrible suffering fate much worse than death?

I didn't know. And THAT is where it began AND ultimately ended for "me"... I don't know.

This book is not wordy or long. It is designed to give you the absolute bare essentials, without dogma or "spiritual" trappings. Just the facts... what is real and what is not real... and the simplicity of the cause, and cure, of psychological suffering.

Perhaps you are not suffering as dramatically as I was. Perhaps your life is Okay, BUT there is a subtle malaise, a nagging sense that something is wrong. Maybe you don't consciously think that something is wrong, but there is a nagging little sense just below the surface, a feeling something is missing, that there is an emptiness you cannot fill.

If you are human, this little book is for you. This book is for all who are interested in being at home and living as natural, fundamental peace, regardless of circumstances... and I assume that if you are reading this, the possibility of being free and at home with yourself and your world interests you.

Whether you are living a life of glee and accomplishment (and under the surface is a fear you'll lose it all) or living a life of either quiet or loud desperation, this book is for you.

My own incessant suffering led me to pursue some bizarre and wonderful disciplines, practices, Gurus, teachings, meditation techniques. For thirty-plus years!

Guess what? None of them worked.

Little did I realize that the end of suffering was closer to me than my breath!

That is, until I happened on the "Non-duality" Teachings coming through the perfectly ordinary and absolutely clear Presence of one John Wheeler of Santa Cruz, California. *John has authored three popular books on this natural non-dual Seeing; see appendix two.*

Meeting with John produced startling clarity; then I found myself being led to meet HIS Teacher, the wonderful Australian "Sailor" Bob Adamson, a man whose own suffering had ended in the presence of the Indian teacher Sri Nisargadatta Maharaj —

many of whose illuminating talks with seekers were recorded in the book I Am That).

Off to Oz

I went to Melbourne, Australia to see Bob in September 2005. Imagine the desperation that led me to travel all the way from California to Australia to seek peace!

Meeting with Bob was a rare treat and signaled "the beginning of the end" of all suffering, as he graciously and generously pointed out the facts of what is Real and what is NOT.

I spent several days visiting with Bob and attending his meetings, and at the end of my visit I knew intuitively that all the questions were answered and I was sure of my True Nature.

I returned to California feeling very grateful and yet there were still little blocks of confusion that seemed to obscure the natural state I had seen so clearly with Bob.

So for a few months, there were phone dialogues with Bob, and with his "graduates" John Wheeler, Brian Lake, Stephen Wingate, John Greven, Gilbert Schultz, Annette Nibley, and Burt Jurgens. Thanks to their compassion and generosity, the last vestiges of doubt were brought out to be seen and looked into; and then finally there was a pivotal two-hour meeting by phone in early July 2006 with John Wheeler. That did it.

What IS Awakening? Self-Realization? Enlightenment?

Good News! There is NO such thing as enlightenment. Instant, clear apperception of this fact is itself the REAL enlightenment, as Nisargadatta pointed out! Enlightenment IS what you Already Always ARE. You can call off the search!

So: I did NOT "become enlightened." There is no such thing as an "enlightened person!" Nor is there any BODY that gets enlightened: The body is made up of the elements... Water, air, fire (98.6 degrees of that), earth (food grows there and feeds the body) etc... That body is meat. And, there is NO "enlightened" MEAT.

What happened was, in a way, nothing. That is to say, what happened is the one who was suffering was seen to be a phantom, an imaginary character, no more substantial than an idea in mind — a thought. And this thought has no power, no free will, and no volition; it is uncaused and causes nothing. It is just an appearance, a will o' the wisp, the phantom of the soap opera called "my" life... all nothing but story.

When the storyteller is seen to be false the whole story is seen to be nothing but a bunch of recurring yet impermanent thoughts, like clouds in an empty sky.

Who's in Charge Here?

I always thought I was "Charles in Charge." The controller and designer of "my" life. Despite the overwhelming evidence to the contrary (car accidents, overeating, doing drugs, drinking and generally "making a mess of things") and the refusing to look at who was really there designing and controlling, I persisted in the ignorant beliefs that "Me, myself, and I" were "In Control."

Even when a wheel broke on my race car in 1968 at 160 MPH and I crashed heavily, injuring the body - and the brain - and bringing a career as a world class race car driver to a screeching, banging sudden stop.

I'm not sure I even began to question that notion that "I" was "In Charge" until my whole so-called life fell apart in 1974 as I lost my business, money, cars, home, wife, even sanity! The whole lot went up in smoke! See the soon to be published book <u>Absolute Freedom</u> for the whole gory story.

After that first meeting with John Wheeler in November of 2004, the whole issue of control began to be seen as a myth, and in the crumbling of that fixation and the attendant suffering, there was also great fear and sometimes despair as the inauthenticity of who I believed myself to be got cracked, little by little.

There is a great story Ramesh Balsekar likes to tell about the California restaurant he visited where they offer a baked potato encased in a clay shell before it goes into the oven. After it was well baked and the shell was hard as a rock, the maître d' of this very pricey place would wheel out the potato on a silver tray on which also rested a tiny sterling silver mallet.

With great pomp and circumstance the fellow would tap tap tap tap tap on the clay shell, and tiny cracks would appear. Then at one more tap the whole shell would collapse revealing the beautiful potato within. That was the way it happened for "me"... the pointers kept tap tap tapping, the Self tapping on its apparent shell, "from the outside AND from the inside out, so to say," and the ever present self shining Presence of the True Impersonal Being-Self then was unconcealed. As that occurs to no one, there is an effortless and totally natural seeing that there never was any designer or controlling entity anywhere to exert its will over the spontaneous unfolding of the aliveness – and life itself.

How is it that the illusory controller seems to persist? Lack of investigation. That is all. Meeting someone who has "gone through the process" so to say (because time itself is another fundamental illusion; where is time unless there is a so-called "thinker"?) can be the beginning of the end (and the end of all beginnings.)

Then the mistaken idea that there ever was a "me" and a "teacher" and "student" dries up and blows away.

And then (now) all there is, is Absolute Freedom.

For No One.

With the pointing to what is Real coming through my friends, it was seen finally that there is nothing to get and no one to get it!

This is the end of suffering: Seeing the falseness of the "me" AND seeing what is always absolutely Real and Present... the sense "I Am," I exist and I am Awareness. More about this later. The bottom line is, you exist and are Aware. That is what you are. There is no separate entity in the human organism. The person is false. That is what you are not.

While I deeply LOVE "Sailor" Bob, Tony Parsons (*despite his tendency to be one-sided and stridently claim his is the only way,*) John Wheeler, Stephen Wingate, Gilbert Schultz, Annette Nibley, and John Greven, let me make clear that none of these people are "Heroes" or "Gurus." These are simply *good people* who found something that works and who share generously from the heart.

In actual fact there is no real "Teaching." And all will tell you, there is no "teacher." They "do" nothing.

No Teacher, No Teaching

I certainly am NOT a teacher or a guru. I am, in this dream-story, *a friend*, one who is moved to share what worked for me to bring the despair of psychological suffering to a complete and permanent halt! In Truth I am nothing. No Thing.

So long as the play, the dream, seems real for the seeker, then the bottom line is that with some pointing to what is actually REAL, AND some pointing out what is NOT REAL, the suffering can end. I was in terrible shape when I encountered these pointers. The end of suffering did not happen overnight. There were physical issues to deal with as well as the mental despair. But ultimately, the pointers sank in and the clarity and freedom opened, sort of from the inside out.

Ultimately, who cares how long it takes? No one. Because in this Timeless Presence Awareness, there is no story, no time, no past, no future, no present. So in actual fact, there never was a process or time span or any of that. Timeless Being IS what is... just that. Period.

Taking It On

The pointers work. That is for sure. Many suffering seekers have been set free, over the centuries... this "work" arises from Oneness itself to bring the seeker back to Oneness... Being – The Home You Never Left.

You may want to take on this book and do the work of looking within as though your life... your aliveness, joy, peace, happiness... depends on it. Because I can assure you from my direct experience, if you are suffering, IT DOES depend on it.

The end of suffering is available right here, right now. The invitation from I Am to I Am is hereby extended. Take it up or not; I know that regardless, you already ARE That... "That" meaning pure Consciousness, Presence Awareness, Being... whichever label for the timeless, inexpressible Being-ness you prefer.

You are invited with love to work with the pointers. And play with the concepts. But do NOT believe any of what you read.

Knowing your True Nature is NOT a matter of belief! It is a direct non-conceptual knowingness that is plain and simple and unfiltered by mental constructs... including the core constructs called "Me-Myself-I-Mine."

The bottom line is simplicity itself: Right here, right now, you know that you are. You exist and you are aware that you exist. That is it... what you have sought is already here, clear and present. That Thou Art.

Don't take anyone's word for anything... DO the work with the pointers in this book, and see for yourself: *You are already free.* You are already abiding as natural stillness, in silence, as peace. Discover this for yourself. Then your own True Nature will (so to speak) "say" in silence, softly, "Welcome Home, dearly beloved. Welcome Home."

> *Your own [True] Self is your ultimate teacher (sadguru). The outer teacher (guru) is merely a milestone. It is only your inner teacher that will walk with you to the goal, **for it is the goal.*** — Sri Nisargadatta Maharaj

Caveat Emptor

This book is a description of an unfolding that happened through an appearance, a body-mind apparatus called "Charlie." The name and form are irrelevant. The happening of this is NOT personal or attainable. It simply happens — or not.

The apparent "exercise" called "self inquiry" described in this book is a spontaneous occurring, often seeming to be a prescription given through instruction. But in Reality it arises through sharing of Oneness with its Self.

The invitation is to allow the resonance of that One Energy to open and unfold through "you"... and perhaps, that "you" will evaporate and all that will be is Awareness, the Absolute, and the Play of Consciousness.

As a British wag notes, "If you are a seeker, I hope you die soon."

Same here.

Obviously (hopefully it's obvious!) that I am NOT advocating suicide! I am pointing to the death of the ego-sense as that which must be seen to be false. That seeing is a dying, in the way the sages from Christ to Lao Tzu to Buddha to Rumi — and so many others — have pointed out over the ages since the beginning of "time.".

Die before you die. Than do what you like. It's all good. – Zen Master Bankei

Part One

From the Unreal to the Real . . .

Pointers from Oneness to Oneness

1. Great Expectations: The Myth of Enlightenment

So you are a seeker, right? You seek the holy grail... absolute permanent happiness, the bliss of a thousand orgasms, the light of a thousand suns, the eternal Light, Brahman, God Consciousness... or whatever other label piqued your fancy that made you say, "Aha! Enlightenment! I want THAT."

Something We Don't Know Made Us Seekers

A note here about "being a seeker:" do you think YOU chose to put yourself through the torture of being a seeker? Think again! A thought arose, a book showed up, a Maharishi appeared on a TV show, he was so charming in his white dress and all his devotees loved him so... something happened, and something took hold of you, and as one sage put it, "Your head went into the tiger's mouth." And when the tiger bites off your head, nobody knows. But if you are like I was, you pray that the tiger bites down and ends the suffering. Because, make no mistake, seeking God or whatever IS pure suffering.

Now you are (let's be honest!) hoping THIS book will "Do It for Me." Right? I know the feeling... been there done that got the t-shirts (a whole bunch of them.) I have good news and bad news. The bad news is, there is NO such "personal state" as enlightenment that any (false) "you" can *ever* attain.

The good news is, there is no such "personal state" as enlightenment that any (false) "you" can ever attain. So you can relax, and quit seeking, right?

Well, maybe not! As you go through this little guide to get from the unreal to the real, you will with any luck at all discover that the whole issue is moot, because... Ta Da... there ain't no you to get enlightened! And all there is already IS the Real.

See, the REALLY good news is, all there already is, is "enlightenment" and you are already that. It's just that "YOU" cannot OWN THAT... because THAT is the absence of the one who wants to own That which is the Real Nature of That.

So what to do? Read the book, try looking in the ways suggested, and take what you get. Then what you may discover is The

Cosmic Joke: There is no one who needs to find God or Source, because the One who is looking IS ALREADY Source.

Listen up: You ARE what you seek. YOU ARE Oneness.

YOU ARE "The Secret Mystery"

As you are, you are That. As you are not, you are That.

There is a notion, quite popular in "spiritual" circles, that the "Great Beings" or "Enlightened Masters" are somehow special and have had miraculous powers bestowed upon them by "Grace" or some other nonsense. Look: There are NO enlightened PEOPLE. There is no "enlightened" MEAT. The body-mind organism is a machine. No more special than a duck, or a tree!

When there is "Understanding," then there is no person who owns that. There is simply LIFE living itself through vast billions of objects, some sentient, some not — in a marvelous phantasmagoria, a profound and brilliant display of light, color, sound, silence, movement, stillness... all appearing right before your eyes in a stunning overload of stimuli that seemingly masks the illusory dreamlike nature of the whole play.

All YOUR own Play of Consciousness.

Unbelievable? Yes. As a belief these word are useless. Look at what the words point to though, and you may see clearly what is Real... and what is not.

For one through whom the Understanding has arisen and ripened, anything is possible; anything may arise in the Aliveness of the present moment of timeless being, and subside.

A Popular Myth: Enlightened Beings Are Never Angry

WHAT "enlightened Beings?" There is NO such animal (or vegetable or mineral.)

Reality: The body mind organism has its functioning in the Totality of all that is. This includes "programming" so to speak... the essential DNA and subsequent conditioning... and if the appropriate stimulus arrives, the response could be anger or any other emotion. So it would be good to drop the idea that anger will never arise. It DOES... but for no one. (That will make more sense later!)

24

This idealized picture of some perfect Master in white smiling beatifically down on his "flock" can be easily dispelled with a little imagination: Imagine you are able to follow one of these blokes around hour after hour. Sooner or later he will have to eat, sleep, and visit the rest room. Guaranteed! Then, you may see through the charade and realize, hey, he is just like me. The Guru act is all a dog and pony show! And it keeps us mesmerized, and apparently "separate" from The Great Master Guru who seems to be SO much holier than we are.

Then there is the ever-popular myth of "Someday." You know this one, right? "Someday I will realize my true nature." One more seminar, one more book (maybe THIS one!) or one more Satsang... one more retreat and THEN "I will get It"... the big elusive IT! Someday.

Lookit: Haven't you noticed, SOMEDAY NEVER COMES!? Where is the future right now, right here? What is this future? Without language, IS there any such thing? Stop and look. Your life... your aliveness... does it happen someday?? Or right now? Have a look... not thinking about it, just sit in your own aliveness and look. Where is someday?

Absent.

Yet the myth persists in the mental story, imagined to be "real," that "I" will "Get It" "Someday." See through this. Then consider the possibility that the Self you seek is already attained here and now. Presently, livingness IS. That livingness, that experiencing IS what you are. This book provides pointers for seeing this for yourself. Don't skip over them... really USE them to realize that you are already free, whole, complete... you are the essence of love and happiness, naturally connected to all that is... because you ARE all that is.

STOP, LOOK and LISTEN — Understand this, stop and really GET this right now: Suffering is Optional.

2. Seeing Your True Nature... The Basics

The Core seeing is contained in this chapter. There will be more and different expressions of it, and other pages to facilitate a kind of looking and seeing, but this chapter has what you need to know and see and imbibe for your suffering and seeking to come to a halt! The basics. There are just TWO POINTS to imbibe. It is very simple!

1. Awareness is present; that's what you ARE.

2. The separate "me" is a myth; that's what you are NOT.

This awareness is obviously present at all times. It is non-conceptual; it is just the natural knowing of your actual ever present BEING.

In short: What you are, IS... Awareness, Presence, the knowing that you are, you exist... translated by the mind into the thought I Am. And what you are NOT is a separate entity, an "I" in a world of "other."

This can be seen easily when there is no one looking. Paradox? Yep.

This game is not to be played by "the individual"... because there isn't one. How can you play if you don't exist as a player? Read on, and allow the game to come to you as best you can... because once these two pointers are seen and imbibed the game of separation – and suffering – is over. Done. Finished. So let's play!

Are you seeking, and suffering? That suffering can end, right now. No kidding.

What ultimately works is simply looking at what is real and what is not... which you can do right now... and the search can end, right here, right now! Take your time with this. There is no rush... in fact to hurry this looking could get in the way. Be gentle and consistent, as best you can.

Do You Exist?

Right now: Check in to your own sense of awareness, and see the natural knowing that you exist and are aware. Right now: Do you doubt that you exist? And that you are aware? No one can deny the fact of his or her own existence. This simple, always present, Awareness of Being IS what has been sought. It is so simple... That is always here now, was never missing, just overlooked.

Have A Look At This

> Ask yourself now: DO I EXIST?
> Yes, I Exist.
> But As What? Do you really know who you are?
> Ask yourself:
> What Am I?
> Who Am I?
> Where is that I?

Inquire Within

Now, have a look, to see if there is really a separate "me" that can suffer... is there a "person" in the organism? Isn't "me" just a *thought*? Who is thinking? Who is looking? Some investigation reveals that the separate person is completely non-existent. Seeing the unreal nature of the "me" allows for an immediate end to psychological suffering.

With some looking, it is seen that awareness is present and the separate person is absent. *Seeing this is not a mental construct. The answer is NOT in the mind!* It is a clear knowing without words or anything else. It just IS. Inescapable and undeniable.

Presence Awareness, Just This and nothing else.

You ARE That...and that's That. Full Stop.

Right here, right now, you know that you are. You can say, or deny, I Am That. Awareness. And whether you say that or not you are still That!

You exist and you are aware that you exist. That is it... what you have sought is already here, clear and present. That Thou Art. Do you doubt that? Fine. Just see that any doubt arises right here within that self-same awareness that you are.

Then what is UNREAL? What is the source and cause of psychological suffering?

The false sense of being a separate person, an "entity," is the root of all suffering. See through that false self-center and the plug is pulled on suffering once and for good.

Right NOW... you can notice. Hearing is happening. Seeing is happening. Breathing is happening. The heart is beating, blood is flowing, and food is being digested. Thoughts are arising and disappearing. Life functions perfectly and effortlessly.

All Life unfolds perfectly... without any controlling entity called "you."

But there is seemingly a sense of a "you," isn't there? What IS this "you" that comes up as a thought, like a voice-over, running alongside or on top of what simply is?

We say, "I See." Yet, have a look and notice... the thought "I" cannot see. SEEING IS. No "I" is needed for seeing. Same for hearing — the thought "I" cannot hear.

What Is A Me? A "Person"?

The idea of a "person," an individual "I" or "me," is nothing but a wave of energy forming into a thought. A subtle sound. Trace that sound back to its source... find the fountainhead. I suggest you look until you find that source; don't give up until you have got down all the way to That Source (so to say) from which the I thought arises. When you do, you'll pull the plug on suffering!

The word "person" comes form

You see, in Reality this person is an empty meaningless phantom character starring in a thought-story without substance or form: Thoughts are utterly insubstantial. And, if there is no awareness of presence, can any thought even arise? No. And without Awareness-Presence, the thought "I" cannot form.

When you are in dreamless sleep at night there is no "I." Yet the Awareness-Being IS. That beats the heart, That flows the blood, and That breathes in and out. So clearly living is simply happening, absolutely independent of "the thinker" and the thoughts of "me, myself, and I."

So what does that say about who you REALLY are?

Have a look... If awareness is prime — and without awareness there is no Being-ness, no Consciousness, no world and certainly no thought of a "me" — then what are you? Clearly Awareness. Just that. Knowing this is natural and spontaneous... and ends the spiritual seeking once and for good!

Ultimately as we noted before the search for "liberation" is absolutely futile and hopeless... because, there is no such thing! And no one to attain it. It's a story told by a seeker — and the seeker itself is part of the story. So obviously no "person" gets liberated... simply because in Reality there is NO person.

But don't believe or accept anything "on faith!" Investigate, using the pointers in this book, and see for yourself: You are Presence Awareness, undeniable and constantly "on." You are not a thought or feeling of a separate me. Look for that "me" and prove to yourself, there is no such thing!

All There Is, Is Consciousness

All IS Consciousness, Presence Awareness, I AM-ness, Aliveness – whatever label you like to use – to point to That which cannot be known or described, yet IS. That is what we ARE. This Presence is the simplicity of what is... all there is, is This.

Nothing is needed, you are already whole and complete, right now, as you are and as you are not.

So allow yourself to be taken over by what you are... Natural Being-Knowing-Loving. Stop now and be as you are.

This livingness is IT. Period.

Directly Experiencing

Here is an example of the Seeing of This Reality, which I shared with my friend Annette Nibley, from my own direct experience — as the pointers were taking hold and freedom opened fully:

The simple knowing that I AM... I exist, and cannot escape that Being-ness... that is it. The big "IT" is just so simple and effortless and... unavoidable. OK, so that IS what I Am.

It follows then that any idea of a me that is suffering then must be illusory. It can't be otherwise, once the conviction is clear that I am Consciousness...

Then even if there is a flip-flopping, a habitual sense I am a me, that flip-flop can't happen unless I AM. Being is Primary. If there is no Being-Awareness, there cannot be any content *of* that Being-Awareness.

I had been focusing on the CONTENT of Awareness and if the content was a clear seeing and a feeling of connection — oneness experienced — then I felt, THAT was Home — and going in and out of Home was a dance between peace and suffering.

The EXPERIENCE of "No Me" was taken to be the Holy Grail, the goal, the attainment that was sought. But in realizing, and Understanding deeply, that ALL experiences are a part of the CONTENT of Awareness and Awareness itself is always and eternally UN-touched... there is the underlying peace. So I had identified content as awareness, and the click! for me is seeing that ALL that arises, is content, including experience and experiencer...

What I Am is awareness. What I Am NOT is any object, feeling, experience, thought, or any other thing that can come and go. What I am is unchanging, ever present, beingness, space-like, clear, nothing. No thing.

Whether there is a Noticing That or not does not matter. That is. Period. Then when there is suffering, there must be a mistake of understanding, a case of mistaken identity... AND once this mistake has been seen AS a mistake it cannot really hold a position of primacy for very long. The Understanding reminds Itself, so to speak... Oh! There it is, mistaken identity again!

What I have noticed in this eternal Now, is that the suffering, when it arises, is seen through almost immediately. Even amidst a painful coughing spell, in the background there is a constant ever-present knowing that it is not happening to "me"... at first it may be taken on board, like "Oh damn, 'I' am in pain and bloody uncomfortable"... but it is short lived.

Understanding Is All

I am seeing what is meant by Nisargadatta's statement, "Understanding is all." With the clear Understanding of what I am, seeing through the false self-center becomes a sort of natural unfolding of Self to Self...

OK, so the bottom line is this... I Am Awareness... the knowing that I exist, I Am. I Am... Presence Awareness. Just That.

I Am NOT the thoughts of me, myself, I, and Mine. Those — thoughts, feelings, story and storyteller — are objects in what I Am and NOT my true nature.

— — —

I shared that with Annette around July 3rd 2006. Shortly afterward I spoke with John Wheeler for a couple of very wonderful hours — and the search was ended once and for all "time."

Give This One a Re-read

This chapter might resonate for you and trigger some deep looking. I recommend reading it again before continuing.

In fact, it might be a good idea to read the entire book three times. You may notice, if you do that, you missed a lot on the first and second readings.

Who is reading this?

Who is asking WHO?

> Only those who have no knowledge of the Source of destiny and free-will dispute as to which of them prevails. They that know the Self as the one Source of destiny and free-will are free from both.
> —Sri Ramana Maharshi, "Forty Verses on Reality"

3. Be Willing To Be Nothing, Know Nothing

You have probably at least glimpsed by now that what is being pointed to here in this book is your own perfectly natural, ordinary, knowing that you are, Presence Awareness.

What you are *not* is a suffering, separate, limited, fearful, little "person" filled with insecurities, anxieties, and frustrations.

To make this absolutely clear may take some rigorous work and earnestness on your part, if you are to "own" this clear Understanding — in a manner of speaking; in actual fact, no one owns anything, but as we pointed out earlier in the paradox of being a "seeker" we use words and concepts to point toward That which is Nameless, Formless, Timeless... the Being that we are.

So let's get cracking, Okay? Here are a few more points to consider...

> Who Am I Anyway? Am I my Resume?
> —'A Chorus Line,' the Broadway musical

What if the great I Am, the sense of a person, a me, is just a thought-story? Just a *thought of a separate* "I"... with an add-on... I Am... and more added on... I Am Me!?

What is all that in Reality? Apart from an idea, a thought, self-imagination... is there a real, separate "me?"

Without a thought story, I still exist. I don't have to THINK I Am to BE. I cannot NOT BE! I DO exist... obviously! But as what? Who or what is this me that exists, and seeks a blissful state of freedom?

Am I what the sages refer to as Self-Shining, Non-Conceptual, Ever-Fresh Presence Awareness? Just This, and Nothing else?

Let's Play Hardball

If I say, "yes, I am That," who is claiming this understanding as a personal attainment? Who is this person who wants freedom, peace, and happiness? Where is it? What is it made of? Is it real? Or imaginary? What is this Me, Myself, this I?

WHO is asking the questions?

What if... every single thing you know and believe yourself to be, is NOT what you are? Do you assume facts not in evidence about the "me" you think of as yourself?

What if your assumptions are based on false premises? What is a false premise? An assumption that a thing is true in the absence of investigation to look for evidence. For example, a discussion about the characteristics of the wife and children of the man in the moon assumes the existence of a phantom, a myth, a believed tale that "There IS a man in the moon."

I Hear You Asking, How Do I Do This?

Here's what will WORK to stay out of the pitfalls of the mind's assumptions:

1. Give up knowing. This is essential for the pointers to take hold within your Being. Give up that you know anything at all. Especially anything about spirituality. Don't refuse to do this. Your openness is essential. The pointers cannot enter a closed mind-system, so believing or thinking you already know or understand what is being offered is the surest way to rip yourself off. Don't do that to yourself. We are up to ending suffering. Let's not sell out the diamond in your heart for the peanuts of stale concepts or memories or beliefs. OK?

2. Don't dismiss anything you come across here without a thorough investigation for yourself. As a wise man, Herbert Spencer, said, "There is a principle which is a bar against all information, which is proof against all arguments and which cannot fail to keep a man in everlasting ignorance--that principle is contempt prior to investigation."

To reject a premise or a pointer out of hand is real ignorance. Don't fall for the mind's assertions that it knows what is being said or pointed out. The answer is NOT in the mind!

3. Be willing to discover you have been wrong about what you know yourself to be and what you know to be real. This book is about moving from the unreal to the real. The discovery of your True Nature will rock your world in a good way, so just let go as best you can, and LOOK from the spaces that are pointed out into your own aware presence.

4. Look at what the pointer is pointing at, not at the pointer. Judging and evaluating the pointers, forming opinions about them, and memorizing the words will all result in a failure to see the space being pointed out. Don't be like the pet cat. If you point out the window, the cat will stare at your finger. It takes courage and commitment to forgo our infinite wisdom and look through brand new eyes at what is. ALL assumptions and beliefs MUST be challenged. Let the challenge take you over; drop the resistance, as best you can.

5. A note regarding so-called Advaita or Neo-Advaita spiritual teachings: If you have been exposed to any of that you will really need to drop them ALL.... all your cherished spiritual concepts must come under fire. Let it happen. Notice if you are hanging on to any belief – for example, "*there is no person who can do anything, so I must not read and look at this*" is a popular one in some circles.

"There is NO person" as a pointer, is fine. But as a belief that limits us, this belief itself will often ensure that the suffering continues! That is how it happened for me, and I damn near committed suicide in that deep despair and frustration.

Ask yourself: Would you rather be right about what you believe and know, OR would you prefer the suffering be stopped in its tracks once and for good?

Ready Set Go

OK, are you set to go? These next few minutes could be the most important minutes of your life, if you take on what is on offer here. I wish the end of suffering for YOU... right here, right now.

Let's Review — Who And What Are You?

Who do you know yourself to be? Thoughts added on to I Am will come up: I am a man, I am a consultant, I am divorced, I am, etc., etc.... look at the whole list and then just DROP all of that, and now LOOK: Do you exist? Are you aware? You know you are, existing and aware, before you think about it. Right? Stop here and NOW. Before there is a thought "I Am" there IS the beingness. Right? Can you see that you always exist and are aware? Before time, before thought, You Are.

Look around the space you are in. Notice what is there in the space. Now notice that the awareness that knows each object in your space is always the same awareness. Look around again and notice; all the objects in your space arise IN that unchanging awareness. They are seen and known BEFORE the mind appends a label to them.

So LOOK and SEE... What is your True Nature? What are the sages referring to as your True Self? Just This: You exist and you are aware. What you sought and needed to know was only ever that.

You ARE That... Non-Dual Presence Awareness. Period.

That is IT. The BIG "IT" is just this simple awareness of Being... I Am. That I Am that I Am is the same I Am that YOU are, and all the sages from Christ to Buddha, Lao Tzu to all the Zen Masters, St. John of the Cross, Ramana Maharshi and Sri Nisargadatta Maharaj — all were the I AM that YOU are. THERE IS NO DIFFERENCE BETWEEN YOU AND A BUDDHA or a Christ. None. You are the very same Being-Awareness-Presence that everyone is. The difference is most don't know that, because they are hypnotized into believing thoughts like "I think therefore I am" or other ideas... IDEAS ONLY... that claim to create a separate entity where none exists.

All down through the ages the sages have declared, That (I Am) and That (Thou Art.) They have repeated over and over, you already ARE what you seek. You are like a fish in the ocean searching for water.

Let's look again at this pointer: Do you doubt that you exist? And that you are aware? No one can deny the fact of his or her own existence. This simple always present Awareness of Being IS what has been sought. It is so simple.... That is always here now, was never missing, just overlooked.

That is all that is needed... simply looking in your own actual direct experience, you cannot say I Am Not. You have to BE before anything can be said or thought. If you are not BEING then nothing else is either.

The world is an out-picturing of your own
Consciousness

— Non-Dual Kashmir Shaivism

So you see, this Being, That which you actually ARE, is the undeniable Presence of the non-conceptual, non-thought, knowingness — I AM. It follows then that your Being is REQUIRED for the world to be. The manifestation does not exist without your being-awareness. You can verify this easily: When you awake from deep sleep, you as the "I Am" and the world appear simultaneously. This appearance cannot happen unless YOU are there (here)... BE-Ing.

Too simple? Yes... for the mind-intellect. The more you try to figure this out the more frustrated you will become. Because, THE ANSWER IS NOT IN THE MIND.

The mind divides Itself up — Oneness onto Manyness — and it itself is an appearing object that is a product of that energy of dividing. The mind can NEVER understand Unicity; for the mind, "unity is plural and at minimum two" (as Buckminster Fuller described it.) Unicity is NOT Two... indivisible, One-Without-A-Second, beginningless, endless, timeless, spaceless.

Simplicity Itself

THIS Is — Simplicity itself. Got it? Reread these pointers and look back behind the eyes, behind the mind, into nothing from nowhere — until you are absolutely certain: *Yes, I exist and am aware — and I see (it is seen) that this ordinary existence-awareness is my own natural state of being, and that awareness has no borders, no center, no beginning, no end.*

Ask yourself, Where does now begin? Where does this Be-ingness begin? Or end? It doesn't. See right now from this that Be-ing is timeless and spaceless, it is the pure Consciousness, the Ab-solute One-Subject-Presencing... don't stop till this is seen. You may notice doubts arise. Fine. What do they arise within? Aware-ness. Thoughts, feelings like "I don't get this"... OK, where do the thoughts and feelings arise? In that Awareness.

Who do these doubting thoughts arise for? "Me." Who IS that "me?" Where is it? Track back to the Source of the "me-myself-I" thought. Find out: Is it real? Substantial? Or is there a phantom in my soap opera?

Any problem seeing that before anything can exist there must be that existence-awareness?

Trust the pointers — they work.

In Summary

What You ARE Is NON-conceptual I AM-Ness, Presence Awareness, Being, always fresh, self-knowing and self-shining, One-without-A-Second, Intelligence-Energy-Cognizing-Empti-ness... Timeless BEING. Just That.

Got it? (Who got it?)

Are you starting to see that there is really no "you" to "get" any "it?" Or NOT?

Yes?

OK, lets move on and get any doubts and questions re-solved!

> The wise man does not strive for anything, not even for Dharma [good conduct and righteousness, etc.] or liberation. He is free from all actions and movements, and also from desire and renun-ciation.
>
> —The Avadhut Gita

4. Look Deeply Into What You Are And Are NOT

- *The thought I is benign and powerless.*
- It's Just a thought.
- The thought I... Is that YOU?

Nothing that can change can be the Presence Awareness, the timeless being, which you are. You have at least glimpsed this by now, yes?

Have you noticed... this "I" thought is not always there? It is a fleeting, impermanent thought form that comes and goes. Remember the last time you were driving, and noticed that there was no thought "I am driving?" There was just... driving, happening?

So the "Driver" is sometimes there, sometimes not. Yet the driving happens perfectly whether "you" are there or not. Stop now and see this.

Then you can look deeper... who is driving the car REALLY? And who is driving the so-called "driver?" Take a good look: What is in control of the machine ("you") that is driving the machine ("car?") Can you find any entity? Or is it all just... thoughts?! And thoughts come and go. They are not eternal, not real, not lasting. And nothing that comes and goes can be the Real.

One basic premise needs to be kept "on screen:" Nothing that comes and goes can be Real. Or to say it another way, ONLY that which never changes can be Real.

So... What is the thought "I"... in Reality?

The Thought I Am is Not The Actual I Am

What is a concept? As in the concept "I am?"
A pointer.
To what?
Nothing. No Thing. Space. Awareness. I Am-NESS without a subject/object "relationship." The NON-Conceptual I Am... Beingness, just That.
A Relative I says "I am" / "You Are." Two-ness.
An Absolute I says "I Am nothing." Silent Stillness Appearing as No Thing.

An Absolute I says "I Am Everything." Silent Stillness Appearing as EveryThing. Oneness.

> *Words cannot describe this Consciousness Absolute. The mind is lost in its majesty.*
> — The Avadhut Gita

The Non-dual Buddhists declare that *Form is Emptiness. Emptiness is Form. These are Not Two...* This is incomprehensible to the mind. This is The Absolute Paradox. The Mystery. Words are futile to say it. This cannot be said.

Yet we say this. I AM is the pointer to I. I is the pointer to No I. Or Universal I. The One I... Love.

That separate "me"... in clear seeing... is seen to be NON-existent. This investigation is NOT a mental "process" however. This investigation is simply LOOKING. Not "Thinking About."

This "looking" is a natural, easy, affectionate investigation, very much the same as seeing happens through your eyes as you drive along and a beautiful seascape is noticed. The seascape is embraced naturally by the seeing, and no "personal see-er" is needed. The "I" is redundant; all labeling by the mind is redundant.

Direct experience of looking will prove... beyond ANY doubt... that this separate I "entity" is simply... ABSENT. NON-EXISTENT. The I THOUGHT then may reassert itself and CLAIM ITS OWN ABSENCE ("I Am Nobody!") But that too is Oneness playing the great game of hide and seek with Oneness. And once these pointers take hold you can no longer buy into the lies the mind seemingly serves up.

> *That which is false troubles the heart, but truth brings joyous tranquility.*
> — Rumi

This is all a Play of Consciousness. Oneness... nothing is really wrong or right unless thinking happens to say so... It is clear here that ALL suffering is nothing more complex that an unexamined belief in a separate I...

Looking dissolves it and all there is, is...

This.
Aliveness.
Paradoxically:
      In LOOKING there is SEEING.
      But there is NO ONE LOOKING
      and NO ONE SEEING.
You see? :-))

The Eye Cannot See Itself

The physical eye cannot see itself. Like that, the Pure Non-conceptual I -Ness — Be-Ing — cannot see Its Self.

What can any thought see? Does the thought "I"actually see? Seeing is happeing. Reading of this text here and now is the seeing. The words-thoughts "I see" are an overlay. That "personal se-er is false. It's just a thought!

Hence: The Self cannot see its Self. Oneness cannot see an object outside itself! All there is, IS its Self...

Consider... Is there any when outside of now?

Consider... The eye cannot see itself... Oneness can NOT see or know Oneness... it IS Oneness... and That Thou Art. To para-phrase Adi Shankara (Viveka Chudamani)... All distinctions are ul-timately false. Neti Neti. (Not That Not That!) Then what is left? Nothing. Then even THAT goes, and all is Oneness not-knowing in Divine Presence. All is That One and since you exist, you are that... and NOT any separate character. NOT.

Some-when around the age of two or three, a strange kind of hypnosis arises in virtually every human organism: The idea that "I" am separate and apart from Others and The World. It began in innocence... mother said, you are Charles, I am mother, and right away separateness as a mental construct was born. The PURE I Am that we always were became polluted, so to say, by the thought... the THOUGHT ONLY... That I am a thing called "I" and added to that, I am a boy, I am ME, sister and mother are not me but other, I am alone, something is wrong, how will I survive? All added on to this core idea of a discrete "me."

Now we are at the crux of the matter of all psychological suffering: The unexamined BELIEF in the concept, the thought "I" or "me". It was pointed out to me by Bob Adamson, and the other Friends, that this root idea is the source and cause of separation. It took a while for this arrogant stubborn ego-mind called Charlie to embrace and trust this. But finally I saw clearly that the false idea and assumption of the actuality of a separate entity called "me" IS the root of all psychological suffering.

I looked into this, thoroughly... and became convinced due to my own investigation that there simply is no such entity as "me." And in fact there never was! It... this "me" or "I" sense... is just an imaginary character appearing in the aliveness of the non-dual Presence Awareness... That I Am that IS, before the mind translates that Pure Consciousness into the THOUGHT I Am.

It Is SO Simple

Look: If this "me" is nothing but a thought, an idea, where is the problem if the idea is challenged? Do you "believe in me?" Let's challenge that belief, OK?

If there really is a separate real "me" in the organism we will no doubt be able to find it. So lets go on the hunt for the "me." Where is it? Look inside right now. What is the nature and essence of this "me" idea? Can you find anything in you that you can say is YOU beyond doubt? Is there anything in there with ANY independent nature or substance, apart from a thought arising presently in the Awareness that you now know yourself to BE?

This bears repeating often: See if there is really a separate "me" that can suffer... is there a "person" in the organism? Isn't the idea of "me" just a *thought*? Who is thinking? Who is looking? Some investigation reveals that the separate person is completely non-existent. Seeing the unreal nature of the "me" allows for an immediate end to psychological suffering.

With some looking, it is seen that awareness is present and the separate person is absent. Seeing this is not a mental construct. The answer is NOT in the mind! It is a clear knowing without words or anything else. It just IS. Inescapable and undeniable.

What Is The Bottom Line?

What you ARE is Presence Awareness... Being, Just That.

What you are NOT is a separate entity. The "me" is a phantom.

And That is That.

This communication is from Self to Self. There is no "Charlie" or "You." All there is, is Consciousness.

This is IT.

It is due to illusion born of ignorance that men fail to recognize That which is always and for everybody the inherent Reality dwelling in its natural Heart-center and to abide in it, and that instead they argue that it exists or does not exist, that it has form or has not form, or is non-dual or dual. — Sri Ramana Maharshi,
"Forty Verses on Reality"

In clear seeing these are distinct... Consciousness as all that appears... and the Absolute, the One-that-cannot-be-seen-or-known... then it collapses into Not Two. I love the pointer, the eye cannot see itself (the I-Oneness, cannot see or know itself.) All knowing requires a split... into knower/known... the mind is that Energy Intelligence splitting one into two — and many and all... as a pseudo-subject... a false authoring entity... the great Divine Trickster. All appearing in the Absolute non-dual Isness...

Know that you are Presence Awareness. Know that you are NOT a separate "person." See the falseness of the idea of "me" once and for good. Then the suffering cannot arise and (seemingly) overshadow what you are.

The Suffering Ends Just NOW

Follow along with this and put yourself in the picture. You will notice how simple the end of suffering actually is!

All "my worries"— about money, health, ending up homeless unless I find work, getting old, feeling insecure and vulnerable, and so alone... only arise in thinking... and as "Sailor" Bob notes, "What's wrong with Right Now... unless you think about it?"

Clearly, none of that exists in the Awareness, the *non-conceptual I Am-ness*... here and now. Only in thinking there is a real, separate "me" can there be worries about a non-existent future. Pure imagination. I SEEM to have an imaginary person in "my" mind... me. But when I look... right now... to try to find this "me," I come up empty. It is just a thought! Like a cloud, it has no actual substance!

A question "Sailor" Bob Adamson likes to ask sheds light: "Who needs to know HOW" (to make life work?)

Go on the hunt for that "one" and you will never find it! Why? It does not exist. Did you need to know "how" to grow the body from the single sperm cell and ovum? Was there a "you" that thought "I am the sperm cell" and did that "you" know "how" to find the ovum, and join with it? And attach yourself to the wall of the uterus?

Come on: A little solid investigation and the whole house of cards collapses! All that is happening is JUST HAPPENING... as the perfect and divine functioning of the Energy-Intelligence that is the unseen substance of all that appears to be. And what about "time?" Is there any when outside of now? Any where outside of here? Who knows this? Or NOT? Who am I?

Now Ask... Who Is Asking These Questions?

(Silence.)

What's wrong with Right Now— unless you think about it?

The sages point out that any separate "me" apart from Presence Awareness... in clear seeing through thorough investigation... is simply NON-existent.

They say this investigation is NOT a mental "process" however. This investigation is simply LOOKING. Not "Thinking About." Looking non-conceptually... inquiring within.

Am I really separate from awareness and others? My body is separate from other bodies, at least it seems so... but what if that is just another thought attached to the "I?"

The thinking "I" mind claims, I Am my body in a world. Is that true?

Really? Is that true?

The MIND says, "I think so. I believe so."

Where is this thinking, believing, and knowing happening? Language. All words pinned to the core belief in a separate "I"... thoughts.

Without a thought who am I?

Who am I?

Who is asking the question?

Your own direct experience of looking will show you that this separate I "entity" is simply... ABSENT. NON-EXISTENT. Yet for some time after this clear seeing arises from nowhere (the Self) often the I story, with all those habit-patterns of feelings, words and pictures that have been repeated for decade after decade, asserts itself, and "I" am back in the soup!

Until it is seen clearly that what I am is this: I exist. I am aware. That is always present, being is never missing, and all the "me" stories that arise and subside do so IN that space of Being-Awareness.

So then, where is any problem?

There never was any such thing as a problem.

It was all simply a case of mistaken identity.

All "problems" are gone in a flash of seeing. Awareness, just that, is what I Am. All else is an appearance in that and has no existence apart from that!

Suffering is nothing more complex that an unexamined belief in a separate I... an entity separate from Presence. On investigation this "entity" is seen to be nothing more than a will o' the wisp... a phantom made of energy, letters, words... all imaginary.

The ghost is not real.

A little looking and there it is: As it always ever was and will Be. Endless Beginning-less Be-ING.

What I am (you are) is Being, just that... Presence Awareness. What I am not (you are not) is a separate personal being-entity.

This is the end of suffering.

> Subject-object thinking seems to cover the natural state (awareness). But without awareness, thinking could not take place. Because thinking appears in awareness (like a cloud appears in the sky), realize that thinking in essence is awareness. Understanding this, thinking cannot obscure awareness.
> –"Sailor" Bob Adamson

In the next chapter we will look at what TIME actually is... keep looking, keep seeing that everything arises in this Presence Awareness that you are.

5. Before Time Is, I Am

I Am. What is this I Am? Is it a word, a sentence? Is it an object? Or a subject? Is it anything REAL? Or not? What about language? It says I Am in sounds interpreted by a human brain to be representative of a real thing... a table is, a bottle is, an ocean is, and "I" Is. But what if these sounds are nothing more than subtle vibrations of energy, the same energy that beats your heart and rotates the earth around the sun and makes the tides come in and go out? Energy, pulsating, alive in itself, formed from nothing into vibrating livingness, breathing through all these bodies, seeing through all these eyes... intelligence-energy, uncaused in itself, known directly here and now in just stopping and seeing the seeingness, hearing the hearingness... just now, Just Being.

I Am. This core thought, and make no mistake, this I Am is ONLY a thought, arises... from where? Have a look right now. Can you locate a source of the thought I Am? No. Then look again: Is the thought I Am the ACTUAL I Am-Beingness? Without thinking I Am you still exist and are aware, right?

Verify This for Yourself

Stop thought right now:
Repeat:

"I" – I – I – I – I – I – I – I – I – I – I – I – I – I – I – I

STOP!
In that STOP did you fall apart? No. Why?

You are NOT the THOUGHT "I". BEFORE the thought I, then I Am, arises, you already ARE! The thought I is only a pointer to the pure Oneness-I-Am. And the pointer is NOT the thing being pointed to (in this case the NO Thing.)

See right now that the word is not the real. And that the word is made up of sound, and that sound is of the nature of vibration, and vibration is a movement of energy. Look at this and you simply cannot believe the thought I is what you are. Then you begin to see, your True Nature is Awareness, Presence, the knowingness of that One-I-Am, Universal energy intelligence, in motion and at rest... One essence, simply this *non*-conceptual, self-luminous, natural, always-fresh Awareness-Presence. *That and nothing else.*

That is the real I Am, before language translates that pure Presence into a concept dividing the Oneness into I am a thing, separate and alone, vulnerable and shaky, insecure and fearful of an imaginary future "when I will get hurt or die."

That thing is always seeking safety and love out there in a world that does not even EXIST apart from the imagination built up on top of the core misunderstanding that thinks the I Am THOUGHT is what we are.

The sages remind us, *from the beginning, not a thing is.* This can be realized directly and effortlessly right now by simply looking: Awareness, Existence, IS... where does this Awareness-Presence START? Does it have any edges? Borders? Where is the center of Awareness? It does not have one. That, Awareness, is free, unbounded, indivisible, and invincible! And when you know that you ARE That, the search is done.

Mind you, the knowing is NOT something known by a knower. The mind divides what is into this/that, me/not me, knower/knowledge. This knowing is not a personal attainment. That is the antithesis of what is being pointed out: Oneness IS the Knowingness, and That is NON-conceptual, BEFORE language, Timeless Being-ness, Endless Peace.

Before Time is, I Am. That I Am, Presence Awareness, IS your true nature. Don't refuse to be what you are. Don't keep pretending to be what you are not (a *limited* "entity.") And what is time? Without a thought or imagination, where is time? There is no time. In Being, time arises as a concept only. Have you ever been away from NOW? Where does NOW begin? Or end? Timeless Being is all there is, and you are that.

What is all that in Reality? Apart from an idea, a thought, self-imagination... is there a real, separate "me?"

> *Go back to that state of pure being where the 'I am' is still in its purity before it got contaminated with 'this I am' or 'that I am.' Your burden is of false-identifications - abandon them all.* – Sri Nisargadatta Maharaj

Without a thought story, I still exist. I don't have to THINK I Am to BE. I cannot *NOT BE!* I DO exist... obviously! But as what? Who or what is this me that exists, and seeks a blissful state of freedom?

Am I what the sages refer to as Self Shining, Non-Conceptual, Ever-Fresh, Presence Awareness? Just This, and Nothing else?

If I say, "yes, I am That," who is claiming this understanding as a personal attainment? Who is this person who wants freedom, peace, and happiness? Where is it? What is it made of? Is it real? Or imaginary? What is this Me, Myself, this I?

WHO Is Asking the Questions?

> *We are That, 'That' meaning the seeming place in awareness where awareness shines out. But in ignorance of the true nature, That we are, that seeming place in awareness is called me or I.*
> —"Sailor" Bob Adamson

Right now, right here, it must be clear... self-shining, ever-fresh, non-conceptual, timeless Presence Awareness... That Thou Art.

> *The body does not say "I." No one will argue that even in deep sleep the "I" ceases to exist. Once the "I" emerges, all else emerges. With a keen mind enquire whence this "I" emerges.*
> —Sri Ramana Maharshi,
> "Forty Verses on Reality"

> *Blessed am I; in freedom am I.*
> *I am the infinite in my soul;*
> *I can find no beginning, no end.*
> *All is my Self .*
> —The Avadhut Gita

6. Your Fascination With Imagination

You think the shadow is the substance.
−Rumi

Imagination. We think of it as something kids or creative people have... children often have their "imaginary friends" (and have you noticed how real they are to the child?) I recall in my own 'childhood story' imagining a fighter plane flying so low I could see the pilot, who smiled and waved at me... except that for me it was NOT imagination, it was REAL. When I told my mother what I had "seen" she made fun of me and clearly did not believe my story. I was FURIOUS, I "KNEW" what "I had seen." Like we KNOW we see a "real world out there" and that we are a "real person in here" inside this body. Rarely do we question these beliefs, despite the suffering that arises for "the person" as a direct product OF these beliefs.

In "The Great Way" (The Hsin Hsin Ming) of Seng T'san, the Sage notes, "the changes that appear to occur in the empty world we call real only because of our ignorance." These changes are no more real than a dream, or a child's fantasy of an airplane or a make-believe playmate.

Ignorance is an interesting pointer: It speaks to IGNORING the real in favor of the appearing imaginary. Stop and look right now: Knowing that you are Aware, Present, here and now, is there a single thing that is real except for that awareness? Looking in direct experience, there is nothing (No Thing.) ONLY in thought-feeling-story, imagination, is there any "world" or "you" apart from awareness.

Don't take anyone's word for this! Look without thinking about it. Look directly in the space-awareness-being that you undeniably are and see this for yourself. It is not difficult. The idea of difficult arises from the idea of a doer, a person who must look and see. This looking is simply a gentle glance with your own innate curiosity to know what is real – and what is not.

Later in The Great Way the Sage says, "Emptiness here, emptiness there, but the infinite universe stands always before your eyes. Infinitely large and infinitely small; no difference, for definitions have vanished and no boundaries are seen. So too with Being and non-Being."

What does this mean? First off, this is nothing that can be grasped or owned by the "person-mind." It is a pointer to That which knows the knower and the knowing... the non-dual Presence Awareness that is ALWAYS so, always here and now, unavoidable and yet unimaginable. THAT Space-like Awareness, That Emptiness, IS our true nature. You innately know this to be true. Only the mind imagines some reality that argues against this insight... and this imagination IS NOT REAL... that is to say, on investigation, it simply falls apart, like a cloud that looks like a battleship simply crumbles in the breeze.

Let the looking be natural, effortless, and authentic and the seeing will naturally flow to what IS rather than what is imagined. You know that you exist. Now know this: As the Sage Nisargadatta noted, *nothing can trouble you but your own imagination.*

> *This is the mystery of [your] imagination, that it seems to be so real. You may be celibate or married, a monk or a family man; that is not the point. Are you a slave of your imagination, or are you not? Whatever decision you take, whatever work you do, it will be invariably based on imagination, on assumptions parading as facts.*
> —Sri Nisargadatta Maharaj

Imagination is simply an unrealistic idea or fancy. And fascination is a state of being intensely interested or attracted.

The habit of belief in a separate me and a world out there keeps the whole dream appearing real; in the absence of investigation the world and me and suffering are all taken to be just what is. BUT when it gets pointed out that this body of assumptions about what is real and who we are is FALSE, a new possibility arises, from the Home we Never Left... the freedom of Being, Oneness, unfettered by imaginary limitations and unencumbered by the sufferings of the fascinated mind.

The False Stands Only Through Non-Investigation

To believe without investigating the veracity of our beliefs and the concomitant blind acceptance of the false is to prolong the appearance of suffering... and as previously noted, suffering IS op-tional.

So if the pointers are beginning to resonate, realize right now that all we see is no more real then the "person" in your TV set reading the news. "He" is nothing but electrons flashing in a tube and if you unplug the TV set , cutting off the energy that makes it appear real, he disappears instantly. Unplug the energy of belief, re-moving the power that seems to give it separate substance, and the suffering is gone.

The "me" can't give you any trouble once it's unplugged!

Then seeing will arise, for no one, that all there is, is Con-sciousness, Presence Awareness... One essence, not two.

Realize The Reality Now

Realize the Reality in the Sage's final words in The Great Way:

"One thing, all things, move among and intermingle without distinction. To live in this realization is to be without anxiety about non-perfection."
And this one:

> Words!
> The Way is beyond language,
> for in it there is
> no yesterday
> no tomorrow
> no today.

Any questions or doubts? For whom do doubts arise? Where do thoughts of doubt or a thinker-questioner arise? Right here, right now, in Presence Awareness! But we can look at a few common issues next.

That which permeates all, which nothing transcends and which, like the universal space around us, fills everything completely from within and without, that Supreme non-dual Brahman... that thou art.

— Adi Shankara

In recognizing presence awareness, there is no "thing" to see, just natural non-conceptual seeing, actually as it is without subject or object. See this and the realization is immediate that what is labeled as awareness or consciousness or mind can never be formulated as either a subject or an object. Being empty of a subject or object, it is emptiness seeing (cognizing emptiness). Emptiness can never be emptied of emptiness, nor can it be filled by emptiness. With that concept cancelled out, only the wordless thoughtless indescribable emptiness remains. Not a vacuum or a void, but a vivid self-shining, self-knowing, self-aware emptiness, like a clear sky full of light. See for yourself. No one or other can do it for you. Immediate simplicity. Continue to see that the seeing is continuous. Any doubt, question, or argument, and the conceptual seeker has appeared again. See that and non-conceptual emptiness remains undisturbed.

— "Sailor" Bob Adamson

Pain is physical, suffering is mental. Beyond the mind there is no suffering. Pain is essential for the survival of the body, but none compels you to suffer. Suffering is due entirely to clinging or resisting; it is a sign of our unwillingness to move on, to flow with life. As a sane life is free of pain, so is a saintly life free from suffering. A saint does not want things to be different from what they are; he knows that, considering all factors, they are unavoidable. He is friendly with the inevitable and, therefore, does not suffer. Pain he may know, but it does not shatter him. If he can, he does the needful to restore the lost balance, or he lets things take their course.

— Sri Nisargadatta Maharaj

7. Yes, BUT

I Doubt Therefore I am

The ego-mind claims: I am my body, after all, it is solidly here, and I know I am this body...

OR

I think therefore I am. I know this. The Thinker is ME... you'll never convince me otherwise. I am the body and the mind, and that's that. So I don't accept any of this.

OK, you seem to have refused to follow the instructions. And it sounds like you have not really been doing your homework and investigating for yourself.

And I thought I was the only one who did that!

But let's have a look at your objections:

You claim, you are the body. But did YOU form that body from the single sperm cell and ovum? Did YOU make the tiny heart and other organs, form the hands and feet? Have a look! Can't you see that this body came into existence independent of YOU? And that until the age of two or three there was not even a "sense" of any YOU in that body?

Let's get real. Where were YOU while all that was happening? Straight answer? You, as an entity, did not exist. Intelligence-Energy, the moving Presence Awareness, forms all the manifestation out of its Self, like the Spider emits the web from herself.

The Self-Same Self-Luminous Awareness that is present right where you are right now has always and ever been present — and forming itself into the ten trillion shapes and forms and stars and universes and bodies, etc. — in the eternal Divine Dance, the Play of Consciousness.

It's YOUR Play... you ARE consciousness... that is all there is. So in the final analysis you ARE the body... AND all the other bodies and objects and space and Timeless Being appearing as Time (Mind) and so on. One without a second!

Yes, all these appear as discrete objects, and you cannot feel my heart beat nor can I feel yours. BUT... there is NO separation of anything from anything else... except in a THOUGHT. No thought, no separation.

And just how real is the mind? Mind is a concept; there is no mind in Awareness. What there is, is thoughts arising in the Sky of Being-Awareness... like clouds. NO thought is real. ONLY No-Thought is real. This is NOT an absence of the appearance of thoughts, simply seeing that nothing about any thought form has any actual reality apart from its essence as Present Being-ness.

This pointer may challenge deep convictions. I stand by this. Do the investigation! See it for yourself. Being awareness, there is naturally a seeing that thoughts arise IN that, correct?

Get this right now. You are existing and aware... Being. Undeniable fact. NO one can deny his or her own existence. IN that existence, Awareness, an idea arises: "I am a schmuck, I should never have quit my job, I am such a loser."

Notice these little dissertations start with "I Am."

Now notice the thought I Am and trash everything after I Am. It's like, I Am, STOP. Dwell in that presence of I Am and see, from where does the thought I Am arise? What is it made of? Let your mind settle down to the Source of that I Am thought. Watch from where it bubbles up. Notice the vibration of energy, as it becomes sound, then forms into letters and words and then strings out into conceptual constructs. All relative to other concepts.

The Answer Is NOT in the Mind

How do we KNOW what I Am even MEANS? We have been told over and over that there is meaning and we hunt for it. But what if what you are is meaningless emptiness... and fullness? Nothing — and Everything? Take a look. See the ephemeral nature of thought, see how insubstantial and devoid of substance it actually is, in your own experience.

Next we will look deeper into the source of, and the antidote for, human psychological suffering.

8. All Suffering Is For A Person And There Isn't One

Note: Some pointers are repeated throughout this text, for the simple reason that repetition works. This chapter contains some of that; I suggest you read it as though you have never seen or heard anything on the page before. Then the pointers can do their work.

Have you noticed? Any and all problems... financial, health, love life, situations like career or work, family... are always and only for the imaginary person called me, myself, and I?

Looking directly into what we call life and living, isn't it obvious that all so-called troubles consist of thoughts and emotions, body sensations and feelings?

Is there inherently anything wrong with all that? When there is the clarity that what you are is Presence, Awareness, Being, Consciousness — whichever label you like — then these thoughts and feelings and sensations, whether pleasurable or painful, simply are appearances in the empty sky of what you actually are.

But if there is a subtle sense that what is happening, is happening to "ME," well, then all that becomes suffering... "I am hurting and I want it to stop" or "I am in bliss and I want it to stay" are equally problematic when there is that imagination that "I am separate from everything else and this is happening to ME."

What Is the Antidote to Suffering?

It is startlingly simple:

First, understand what you are: Do you exist? Are you aware? That simple awareness of being is "IT"... your true nature. It is just that simple. Seeking anything beyond this is just the mind wanting more or better, something more spectacular. Just know that what you are is this ordinary being-awareness and at the same time know that any "more" or "better" or "different" is only imaginary mind stuff and NOT what you are! Then stop and see that the answer is NOT in the mind! You already ARE what you sought in meditation, chanting, sitting, doing "Seva," (service to a guru, a great way for the guru to keep expenses down!) and making endless pilgrimages to satsangs and gurus and all that. JUST STOP. You are ALREADY what you sought.

Presence Awareness. Just That.

You Are That. Nothing Else.

Now, looking within the space of awareness, see if you can find any separate entity, any "me" as a real, substantial object... apart from a thought or idea of an I or a me or a sense, a feeling. Is that sense or feeling what you actually are? NO. See this right now and suffering is over. It is only the belief in separation that causes suffering. Root out that belief by looking, investigating.

Don't dismiss the possibility without looking for yourself. This is NOT a philosophical matter; it is a practical, hard hitting way to see for yourself what the cause of suffering is and tear it out at the root. The me thought has NO substance or independent existence apart from the steadily self-shining awareness it arises within... and in looking closely at that "me sense," it is seen for what it is... A PHANTOM, an ephemeral, imagined self center that never actually existed at all!

> "Actions happen, deed are done, but there is NO individual 'doer' thereof"
> — The Buddha

See the insubstantial, cloud-like nature of the "Imaginary Person" and the game is over. Then there is the natural celebration of the livingness that powers all these bodies and plants and universes and is of the nature of absolute unconditional Love.

Then there is the welcoming back to the home you never left.

Right here, right now, it is all clear. You are freedom itself, unlimited and non-conceptual, fresh and new in every moment. And you do NOT have to practice meditation, or other techniques, to be what you are. In fact, practices can keep you back! We'll look at that idea next.

9. What About Practices?

Given the fact that being-awareness is what we already are, and that it is never not present, what could a meditation practice accomplish?

Only obscuration of the ever-present being-awareness. A practice engages the mind, and that seemingly obfuscates our simple ever-fresh presence of being. We go into the mind to transcend the mind. How could that ever work!?

The best practice is NO practice — but there is in fact no one to either practice or avoid practicing, in the Presence Awareness that we are. So don't take this as some advice to stop meditating or chanting! If you like it do it. Just realize that NO practice can lead you to what you already are. How could it? Seeking what you already are is like looking for your keys in the living room when you actually have been told you left them in the kitchen by a trustworthy friend who saw you do that.

The sage points out the futility of looking for What Is where it isn't as the same sort of foolishness. You are what you seek. So whether you start OR stop a practice is irrelevant.

The answer is never to be found in that mind-stuff. Seeing that, then we naturally eschew any movement out of presence with a mental exercise.

Some practice may come up. No problem.

But the end result is almost inevitably going to be frustration, because any state achieved during a practice is temporary, and when it fades you are right back where you started from!

I learned that one the hard way, after thirty years of engaging the mind in practices, overlooking the simple being-presence that was and is always right here right now!

So the solution to the question of practice, for me, came when I began to ask, who is practicing? Where am I trying to get? What am I right now? Why do I need to change? If I am suffering and trying to change that suffering to a peaceful state, have I looked at what I am before beginning a practice? Who am I? What is it that is suffering? What am I trying to attain? Is that even real and attainable?!? Who is looking, asking, seeing, and hearing?

Looking into the space, for who I am — and for who is asking who? — leads naturally to a seeing that what I am is nothing. Not a thing — and yet, I am here. I exist. I am aware that I exist. And that is clear and unfettered and needs no practice to "get to." It just IS. Always, Here and Now.

Then what is this me that wants to change or alter or correct this simplicity of what IS? On the hunt for that me I find it to be totally absent... and the whole paradigm of practice, practicer, and goal of practice just goes poof! And then...

There Is No One To Practice; There Never Was

This is not to say that along the way, the dream character may not be led to partake of a meditation practice... but once the hook is seen, the practice simply loses its appeal, because it is seen that any practice reinforces the sense of being a separate individual who can "attain" some "state"... and once this is seen the jig is up on that dream-practice.

> Until you are free of the drug [of self-identification], all your religions and sciences, prayers and yogas are of no use to you, for, based on a mistake, they strengthen it.
> — Sri Nisargadatta Maharaj

> You impose limits to your True Nature of Infinite Being. Then, you get displeased to be only a limited creature. Then, you begin spiritual practices to transcend these nonexistent limits. But if your practice itself implies the existence of these limits, how could they allow you to transcend them?"
> — Sri Ramana Maharshi

> There are NO non-dual practices.
> — Gilbert Schultz

Perhaps, practice makes IM-perfect. "We" shall see — when there is no see-er.

10. Suffering Is Distinct From Pain

Pain Happens. Suffering Is Optional.

Suffering and pain are distinct.

How?

Basically, pain is a signal that something is not working in the organism. Dogs have pain. Humans have pain. But the dog does not suffer — because the dog does not have a sense of being a sepa-rate psychological entity that takes ownership of the pain— and as the owner, that entity adds the secondary idea that the pain "should not be."

The sage Nisargadatta Maharaj pointed to this perfectly. Late in his life his body was wracked with pain from cancer. One time a visitor asked him as he saw him wincing, "Maharaj, are you in great pain?" The sage replied, "There IS great pain."

This is quite illuminating when looked into. "There IS great pain" acknowledges a condition of the body but makes no claim to owning that pain. In Presence Awareness, anything can arise. But it is NOT "taken on board." When Charlie's back or arthritis hurts It is not MY pain. There is no suffering unless there the FASLE me-mine split in the thought-story.

All that arises is simply what IS... and is not a personal mat-ter. Once it is seen that what we ARE is Presence Awareness and what we are NOT is "an individual," the game is over; you can no longer believe that pain is personal – any more than you can believe the earth is flat.

It may take some deep looking for this to be seen... especial-ly if there is severe pain. For example, being wracked by spasms of coughing may seem to take the attention so completely to the body that the awareness appears to have been "forgotten." But in actual fact is the awareness ever really missing? No. It cannot be.

Possibly what is needed in these instances is to look, as soon as possible, into what it is that is in pain or suffering about there being a wracking cough. We say or think, "I am coughing. I am in pain." We add on to the awareness "I Am" and say I am in pain. Making a sharp distinction between this "I Am" awareness and that which has pain... the body-mind organism... does the trick.

When the sword of razor sharp discrimination is brought to bear on this business of the thought story "I am in pain," then it is seen... effortlessly... that FIRST is I. I is just Awareness. Oneness. I-I, as the sage Ramana Maharshi referred to it. Then next comes I AM... Awareness, arising as Consciousness. Pure knowingness, no subject-object split; just the knowing Existence Is and I Am That.

THEN comes the mischief made of the thought machinery... the mind. The MIND says I am this BODY, and that is taken on board by the I Am as a belief in something real called "my body."

That's the trigger for suffering, as the mind adds on, "I am in pain, I don't like that, I want that to change, why is this happening to me? Poor me! Etc."

Notice that all this is pinned to a core belief in the identification with the body! And yet, where is the body except in a thought story appearing presently?

Making the distinction between the pure I Am, Awareness-Presence, and the thoughts that arise IN that Awareness, makes all the difference in seeing that while there may well be pain for one who has seen his or her True Nature, there is NO suffering, because suffering is only possible for the fictional person. Once that "person" has been seen to be nothing more than thoughts, based on a belief in a separate "me" thing identified as a body with a name, etc., the game is over.

The End of Suffering

When you find out that the earth is round you no longer buy into the story that you dare not sail out too far or you'll fall off... once you know beyond doubt that the phantom is a ghost and is not real, the energy of belief no longer goes into that phantom "me" and its stories. *Therein lies authentic freedom from all psychological suffering*

The end of suffering is simple: Investigate who sees, who thinks, who you are, and see the false nature of the "one who suffers." Then remain as you are... Presence Awareness, just that. Simple and natural. Home.

11. A Review: What is Real? What Is NOT Real?

The Infinite IS, Is That Which YOU ARE

The Identified Pseudo-Subject Is What You're Not.

The One who Knows that this text is being read, registering within your own awareness, IS the One we have been seeking since about the age of two or three.

You are Here, talking to You, the Love that You are. Not the you that thinks I am this and that. This is you sharing with yourself. The speaker and listener are YOU as you are. SEE this by Looking.

Perhaps you have sought that joy, like this body-mind organism called Charlie, in drink or drugs, in sex, or fast cars, or work. In fame and danger. In the approval and acceptance of other people. In Churches, Temples, Meditation, and endless Satsangs, Gurus and Teachers and so-called sages, in seminars and workshops... and on and on. Ad Infinitum. And all the while That Timeless Love watches us, so to speak, seek It "out there," hoping to "someday" find It, and never again lose It.

Someday.

It leaves you exhausted, all that looking for Love when and where it doesn't actually exist, doesn't it?

That awareness that is registering these very words is it. These words and images and spaces on the page are IT. The one who understands is it. The one who does NOT understand is it. The separation and dualism of that separateness is it. The unity of all things is it.

There is nothing that is NOT it.

EVERYTHING is IT. This is the Mystery. This text is all simply pointing you back to your Eternal Essence. You *are* that impersonal empty awareness that sees and hears, AND all that appears within That. You have never *not* been That!

Look. Right Now. Are YOU thinking? Or do thoughts simply arise in the awareness?

Do the eyes see? Do the ears hear? Or is there a seeing happening THROUGH the eyes, hearing THROUGH the ears.

Thoughts are arising in the Space. Notice this. Just stop and look. The One you have been looking for is the One who is LOOKING right now, this very instant-before-time.

You are that. And that is an ocean of awareness-love-freedom. Pure naked possibility arising as Unbounded LOVE.

What If

All there is, is the Presence, Awareness, BEING, IN WHICH the thought "I am" APPEARS like a cloud in the clear sky?

And then some mechanism in the program grabs that thought "I am" and unconsciously turns a thought into an IDENTITY, a ME?

In some circles this BEING or AWARENESS is described as "Non-Conceptual Awareness, before time, just Cognizing Emptiness."

Can any of us say "I am NOT?" There must be AWARENESS to even be able to recognize the thought "I am" OR "I am Not."

Now look: Can any thought appear if there is NO awareness FIRST? Possibly, that *a priori* awareness OF thought and experience and all the rest of it IS the True-Nature the sages point to.

Maybe the CONCEPT or THOUGHT "I Am" is NOT That I AM-ness that PRECEDES thought.

If so, herein lies the source of all problems, the source of all suffering: I think that I am the thinker, not the Awareness IN WHICH the thought arises from NOTHING.

What if we MISTAKE the CONCEPT "I am" for the Space-Like Awareness of pure *a priori* "*I am Ness?*"

What if that I Am IS NO Thing (nothing)... a nothing that is the pure potential for everything?

Maybe, if we have no DISTINCTION between Concept or Representation (Re-Presentation) and the thing itself then we are deluded and ignorant, and we don't even KNOW that we are ignorant.

I suggest here that we mistake the Menu (Concept "I am") for the Meal... the actual SPACE... Pure Pre-Cognitive *a priori* I Am-Ness, the *Oneness from which all that is arises, as its own Self Expression.*

When One is Nothing That is Known by No One.

The pointer is, "The CONCEPT I am is NOT the true I AM."

When this is seen there IS no one and nothing. THAT is the "I AM That" or "That Thou Art" that the sages are pointing to.

What if our starting from the assumption "I am a separate person (me) that thinks and feels and experiences and does all sorts of things" IS the root cause of suffering? This may be nothing more than a BELIEF in a thought-form that is only a representation, NOT that which is being represented.

What if we start from "I am that Awareness IN WHICH all thoughts, feelings, experiences, etc. arise?" Then perhaps the effort to "become" that pure I Am falls away in the realization that we already always ARE That. Then (actually NOW) what is left is the No Thing that we are eternally. The ACTUAL NON-thought NON-feeling, I AM. Simplicity Itself.

Have a look. Really, take a good long look. Do you exist? Can you claim you do NOT exist? Who KNOWS that existence IS? Simple awareness, knowing without an entity that "knows," might then be seen.

Your Psychological Suffering Ends Here

In the final analysis (of nothing by no one) it is seen clearly that "one" cannot "access" what has never NOT been so. THAT which you are is Always Already shining — it is the Light that illumines the mind. Like the Prism and the Sun.

The Mind is like the Prism — notice how much that sounds like PRISON? — that apparently splits the Sunlight into a magnificent display of Color that has NO independent reality without the Light of the Sun.

You Are The Light Of The All The Universes

Without the Pure Unconditioned Light of the Space-Presence-Awareness of the One-without-a-second, the mind cannot BE. IT has NO independent existence: IT is a REFRACTING dividing mechanism – an OBJECT – like the prism is an object.

Without the Prism there is only Light. Without that Light there is Not One Single Thing. Period! End. Stop.

The Light IS all there IS. Form or Formless, it's all That. What we call a human being is NOT a "Subject" that "Observes" "OBJECTS."

The human thing is a body-mind object – a "perceiving object."

This perceiver-object perceives perceived objects! That is all there is in manifestation: objects. Time? A thing. Space? A thing. Body? Obviously a thing. Mind? A thing. Self? A thing. Others? Things.

No thing can exist without that Source, the Light of Presence Awareness. Any more than a hologram could "exist" without the Laser. Or the Shadow could exist *without* the tree that casts the shadow AND the Light that shines and "causes" the shadow of the tree.

You Are That Light of Presence Awareness, shining before and through the mind. Beyond doubt, you exist and are aware. That simplicity, the simple ordinary wakefulness that is always wherever and whenever you are, is IT.

That Is That.

Got it?

If YES, welcome to Being – The Home you never left.

If NO, reread this book, slower, and do the investigation as though your life depends on it. Because, for a life free of suffering... IT DOES.

A Sage once said:

> If a Human Being does not find his True Nature, he has sold a diamond for the price of spinach.

"Get it" or not, "Know it" or not, YOU ARE THAT. Full Stop.

12. After Seeing The Obvious, What Then?

After nothing happens to no one (so to say) the appearance of "residual" habits of thought that have been embedded in the brain cells by years of repetition can still arise.

Once the Non-Conceptual Understandings... the so called pointers... have been imbibed fully, these pointers can immediately arise on the heels of the repetitive thought-patterns and cut them adrift at the root... because the root of habitual patterns of thought and feeling depend on the core "I" thought for their existence.

When the root is severed its branches must – eventually – wither and die.

See that even all these so-called habits are nothing substantial in and of themselves. They're just pure Absolute Presence Awareness arising as energy-intelligence, patterning into sounds and forming letters into thought-words... concepts referring to more concepts, all branching out from the root. See that root – the "I" – as false.

As energy is no longer fed to false beliefs, nor to the false believer – the "I" – they just fade back into the Cognizing Emptiness. They die, as any unfed "thing" dies.

No energy – no life. Have you noticed? Unfed bodies die eventually. All "things" come only to pass... not to stay. All that stays is no thing / every thing. Not Two.

The Absolute alone (all one) IS.

That arises AS Aliveness, which manifests as all there is, including the ideas of separation and completeness, ignorance and enlightenment... everything.

Unicity. That alone IS. This cannot be known... it is no more possible for any "one" (which requires the existence of the concept "other") to know That, than it is for the eye to see itself or the ear to hear itself, as all there is, IS That.

Period.

Tat Tvam Asi.

Remember, the entrance door to the sanctuary is inside you.
–Rumi

13. Zero Degrees of Separation

There is a popular concept that all people on Earth are separated by "Six degrees of separation."

As I am driving my car on the freeway (so to speak; driving is actually just happening, as everything just happens as the dream-manifestation unfolds itself naturally) there it is... the seeing.

Unlike the "spiritual concept" very popular with seekers, which declares, "I am One with Everything", there simply is NO separation, no "I" to BE "One with everything" and no separate "Everything" to BE "One with." Separate everything? To be One With? That concept is utterly oxymoronic.

All there is, is This... Presence Awareness, and nothing is actually separate from anything or anyone else, unless a THOUGHT of separateness happens to arise within that Self Same Awareness as an ASPECT OF That.

To paraphrase my dear friend "Sailor" Bob, *where is any separation without a thought?*

All apparent separation is insubstantial and on investigation, naturally seen as NONEXISTENT. Where is separation in deep sleep at night? The mind-thought-feeling machinery is in abeyance, yet there is a knowing that sleep happened when consciousness arises in the always already Awareness, that wakes itself AS Consciousness, and all the content OF Consciousness.

There is a distinction to be made between Consciousness or Wakefulness, as IMPERSONAL Knowingness.

The One Is All There Is

Whether That is experienced by a seeker or not, matters not in the least! Because, look, what could possibly be excluded from The One Without A Second?

It's dubbed NON-duality. Not two. Where is there any room for a subject observer and an object observed in That? It is impossible.

The seeing of this is natural and effortless as the inquiry is rigorously and earnestly pursued: Who Am I that claims in thought (and thought ONLY) to be "One with everything?" It is the ubiquitous yet totally FALSE sense of a subtle separation, and once that separation is seen to be what it is: Nothing but a thought arising in Awareness Then the jig is up.

> *Oneness is like the clear blue sky – everything arises, unfolds, and subsides within its all-compassionate love.*
>
> *Oneness is our real Self. Everything is an aspect of Oneness. And our quest to know this comes from Oneness.*
>
> — Abhinavagupta,
> on the teachings of
> Non-dual Kashmir Shaivism

Here is a metaphor for this Natural Seeing: It is like, if you are cursed with cockroaches in the kitchen, if you go in there in the wee hours and turn on the light, they scurry away out of sight.

Turn the Light of your very own Presence of Awareness on the mind-thought-and-feeling mechanism, investigate and inquire within to seek the source of the "mind" — and it will scurry away. In a way of speaking only — actually it will be seen, by no one, that it never DID actually exist as a separate "thing."

Now, the pseudo-subject — the I thought — can no longer attach to Consciousness and fool itself into believing it is real.

In That, Pure Awareness, the One, there is NO subject and NO object. All IS as it IS... Not Two.

Don't believe a word of this though! All words are ONLY pointing to That which cannot be expressed in words, feelings, visions, ideals, or any other "thing." All "things" are products of language. Eschew language and there is the True Self, and then you are as you really are... Being, abiding as That and nothing else.

> *The duality of subject and object and trinity of seer, sight, and seen can exist only if supported by the One. If one turns inward in search of that One Reality they fall away. Those who see this are those who see Wisdom. They are never in doubt.*
>
> — Sri Ramana Maharshi,
> "Forty Verses on Reality," v. 9

14. Ignorance at Its Most Elegant

Many philosophers and seminars on "transformation" have asserted, "Language is The House of Being."

This is ignorance at it's most elegant... so to say.

On direct examination: Does language exist in deep sleep? NO. Clearly then, language cannot be the "house" of anything... except concepts. And what is real, actual, again on investigation? NON-Conceptual Self-Aware Being-ness, before any THING... is. And language is a thing.

In deep sleep what is there? What exists? No thing. And that no thing, Being-Presence as sleep, is devoid of "Consciousness" which arises only when no thing stirs itself into form and formlessness as its true nature of stillness-silence throbs in Loving to BE and the body mind apparition arises as a conceptual so called "entity... with language."

Sleep well, we say. Who sleeps!?

Notice that (don't just believe it) unless there is 24/7 Beingness, can there possibly be ANY arising of anything?

That simple beingness is the "Source" and the "Manifestation" — rising out of no thing — of all "relative states of consciousness."

Waking, dreaming, and deep sleep MUST BE an ASPECT of that "Presencing– Awaring" No Thing. The Absolute could care less: It stands alone as all that is... supremely free and untouched by any appearance, yet — paradoxically — Being the Source of all appearances.

Apperception of this pointer is essential.

Without first there being existence itself, can any "thing" exist? And as it is seen that existence itself is no thing, then: Can any "thing" come out of "No Thing?" Or is any "thing" (including all things) simply an "expression" of, or an "aspect" of, nothing? And bingo! All appearance is substantially nothing; Nothing is all that is. Nothing-ING. Life its Self, arising as alive-NESS. Aliveness Be-ING.

Take a seed from an apple. One seed. Now open it up. What is there? Bits of seed. Take a bit and take IT apart. Look for the tree. Where is it. Yet the intelligence of creative energy, itself an arising out of that No Thing, will often – not always! – sprout into a mighty tree with copious leaves and abundant apples, when planted correctly!

Look into a seed. Take it apart

Where is a tree in a seed!?

Dismantle the last bit of the bit of the seed. What's left?

The Source and the substance of a tree. That Thou Art.

This may be understood with intellect first. Okay. Now ask that intellect, who are you that says, "I know, I understand?"

Find that "understander." Have a really good look.

Oops.

It's absent.

A Ripple In The Pond

The ripple has no separate or independent substance – no existence – apart from the pond

Both ripple and pond are water, appearing separate. That is simple enough to see. –if there is a willingness to suspend "what I know" and actually LOOK.

Understanding as a mental comprehension comes and goes. The Knowingness is a natural non-conceptual seeing. In seeing there is no seer or seen, only ordinary seeing – *just* the seeing.

Subject/object duality is not real in No Thing. These are only ideas held by that "entity with language" that has falsely taken charge – or so it seems to a trapped mind still convinced of its own independence from all that is – and it's supremacy.

It is a con job.

Albeit a "divine" con job, so to speak... obviously it cannot appear in the absence of the Absolute, for which another label could be "Divine Being."

Delete the word divine and what's left? Being. And that, silence-stillness, before consciousness and space-time, is Source – another label.

Don't get caught up in all these words! Look and see: Is there a separate entity OUTSIDE of language itself!?

We say "I am a man or a woman." That is the identity claiing that IT is a body.

Without language where is any body or mind or world?
Find out.
Who owns the body mind world complex?
Me?
Thee?
If you find either one bring it to me.
Good luck!

Love What You Are

Love what you are as it is and seek only the source of language: "Who speaks?" "Who writes?" "Who reads?" Who is the "me" if there is only no thing in deep sleep yet Aliveness, Presence Awareness, arising as Energy-Intelligence, beats the heart and creates new cells and destroys old ones, grows hair, fingernails, and breathes air into and out of the lungs.

Who Am I!? Who???

Look for yourself until it is seen that there is no "myself."

And have fun with it! If you like, you can e-mail and let me know how it unfolds itself – from an is-person to no-person to all that IS. Everything. And No Thing.

Again, don't believe a word of this. It is language attempting to point back to Source, and no words are TRUE! Do the homework and find that out; don't simply accept it as another piece of baggage to carry around and repeat at seminars and satsangs!

> *Whereof one cannot speak, thereof one must*
> *remain silent.*
> — Ludwig Wittgenstein

Go deep.

15. 'How Do I Know When I'm Done?'

I once asked "Sailor" Bob Adamson, *How will I know when the seeking is finished and I am all done? I am sick and tired of being a seeker!*

There is another oxymoron. What I wants to be done?

But I do remember that space well... god, when is the tiger gonna chomp down and take off the head that seems to cause SO much suffering!? "Sailor" Bob and John Wheeler dealt that sucker a death blow! Thanks be to Nothing!

The answer is useless as a remembered "affirmation" because the one who affirms, the one who wants the seeking to end, the one who is sick and tired, simply does not exist as a fact but only as a believed-in entity called "I" or "me." That false belief then gives rise to the inevitable belief that there is OTHER than "I." And it all gets endlessly added onto from that basic misconception.

The suffering seeker is no more real than the man in the moon is real. Who ARE you? Look for the "one who thinks he suffers! The one who wants it to end. The one who is frustrated." Until the inquiry is taken on in earnest it can never be seen that there actually IS no "person who suffers." Then it's all over.

The bottom line is this: NO "Me" or "You" will ever know "when the seeking is done." When there is no one to ask the question, the question never comes up again. Because the questioner is gone and all there is, is Presence Awareness, arising as all that appears to be.

Who are you? And who is asking, "when will I be done?" Dig deep in the space of the natural knowing that you are always and only Presence Awareness. Starting from this, ask what thinks or believes otherwise?

Inquire!

Who Am I?

Being committed to freedom, investigate the identity with that question.

Who Am I?

Don't stop until there is no one to either *do* or *not do* this.

16. The Cleaning Lady Is A Sage

A Tall Tale from the Sufi Tradition, Westernized by the Author

Once Upon A Time, the White House hired a cleaning lady, ancient, shriveled and bent. Her duties were to include cleaning the Oval Office in the wee hours of the morning. Unbeknownst to the Chief of Staff or anyone else in the House, this old crone was a True Sage. Ordinary in appearance, nothing special, just an elderly cleaning woman.

One night there was an alert that required the President to come down from the residence to the Oval to meet with a special delegation that would be arriving at four AM. The Assistant Chief of Staff decided he'd better check to make sure the Office was ready for the President and his visitors.

Opening the door, he spotted the old woman asleep in the President's chair, her feet up on the desk, snoring loudly.

"What the hell are you doing?" He shouted. "Who do you think you are to be sitting in the president's chair?!?"

Yawning, the old lady smiled at the Assistant Chief and said nothing.

Even angrier now, the Chief yelled, "I said, who do you think you ARE to sit there? Do you think you are the Majority Leader or something to be sitting there??"

"No," the crone murmured softly, with a very kind look in her eyes. "I am much higher than that."

"WHAT!? Higher than a Majority Leader? I am the Assistant Chief of Staff. Do you believe that you are higher than ME? Do you think you are the new Chief of Staff here?"

"No. I am much higher than that, sir."

"Well, higher than the Chief Of Staff in THIS place is only the President Of The United States! Do you think you are the PRESIDENT?!?"

"Oh, no sir. Not at all. I am MUCH higher than THAT."

Smiling sweetly, she spoke with a clear deep voice that evoked a silence that was all but unmistakable. But the man missed that Silence and continued to rant.

Now the man was truly outraged. "WHAT!!?? How DARE you, madam! I demand that you recant. Higher than the President is only GOD. DO you think you are GOD??"

Laughing aloud, she said "Oh, of course not, dear boy. I am MUCH higher than GOD!"

"Higher than GOD? NOTHING is higher than GOD."

"Ah. Now you have it, dear boy. I AM that NOTHING."

> *If the ego is, everything else also is. If the ego is not, nothing else is. Indeed, the ego is all. Therefore the inquiry as to what this ego is, is the only way of giving up everything.*
> — Sri Ramana Maharshi,
> "Forty Verses on Reality"

17. The End Game

The last stand of the mind is found in the zeal for the co-opting of the fact of Being No Thing into someone who OWNS that... thereby seemingly becoming "somebody who knows they are nothing."

This is the trap of the fabled "enlightened ego." The claim by an entity that there is no entity!

There can be great intellectual "clarity" about what is real and what is unreal... but as long as "Someone" OWNS that "clarity" then you can be sure that the Final Truth has not revealed itself. Because this Understanding IS NOT A PERSONAL MATTER. This cannot be stressed too much... a common pitfall in the unfolding of non-duality is this notion that "Aha! Now I am enlightened." One does not have to look far to see Satsang teachers claiming this enlightenment and offering to "teach" others "how to get enlightened."

That is spiritual arrogance.

How can anyone teach you to BE?

It would be as though I was claiming to be able to teach you how to beat your heart and digest your food. It's utter nonsense at best and an often expensive con game at worst.

You ARE. THAT is indisputable! If there are vestiges of identification with the body or mind, with thoughts or feelings, then BE YOUR OWN GURU. Look within. Inquire: Who Am I?

Don't stop until you see beyond ANY doubt that the thought-form "I" is a FALSE entity. The "I" thought is NOT real. It has no existence apart from the Awareness that you are. If identification seems to persist, keep looking for the SOURCE of the I thought. From where does it arise? What is its substance? Does it have any independent nature apart from the Awareness that you are? Does it have any mass or shape? Doesn't it come and go? And can anything that comes and goes be ultimately real?

No.

ASK: Who Am I?

You are not looking for an answer or outcome! This is an objective investigation, like looking into the innards of a clock to see what makes it tick.

Bring forth the questioning: Who Am I? And Who is asking this question?

Who am I?

This investigation happens naturally when the zeal to find "the right answer" is forsworn and the looking is just a simple peering into the space, as one might peer into a dimly lit room to see what is there.

Keep at it as long as there is any sense of separation left. Allow the answers to float up and disappear; don't hold to ANY answer. Answers are concepts and NOT real. They are just thoughts appearing and disappearing, devoid of substance, unreal in essence. Appearances. Phenomenon.

What IS real is Noumenon. That which cannot be known through perception, although its existence can be demonstrated... i.e. by the absolute FACT that existence unarguably IS.

Do the inquiry as long as there is ANY subtle sense left that "you" are a separate "do-er." Discover once and for good that the I thought is as insubstantial and powerless as a cloud in the summer sky. Let the Light of Awareness shine through that cloud. Watch as it dissipates. Naturally, as your own Awareness of Presence shines as the light of pure knowing and reveals all the thought stories to be as dreams, with no power and no actual reality.

Who Am I?

When there is no answer, there is no question... and no questioner.

<u>Who asks the question?</u>

Then it is seen, that question and question-ER are one essence, energy forming into sounds letters words concepts. And YOU are not that.

<u>Who asks the question?</u>

And there is the Silence that You Are.

Be still and Know... I Am.

That.

Not Two

Not One.

Just This, As it Is.

WHO?

Who Am I?
(No answer)

Who Am I?
(No answer)

Who Am I?
(No answer)

Who Am I?
(No answer)

Who Am I?
(No answer)

Who Am I?
(No answer)

Who Am I?
(No answer)

> *Take the idea "I was born." You may take it to be true. It is not. You were not born, nor will you ever die. It is the idea that was born and shall die, not you. By identifying yourself with it you became mortal."*
> —Sri Nisargadatta Maharaj

18. The Cosmic Game of Hide and Seek

A Fable

Once upon a time there was No Thing, bubbling as joy and peace. Unconditionally Loving To Just BE.

Then for sport That created boredom. Now, it was boring being nothing, and everything. So the One split itself into two, three, seven, forty four, many more, millions zillions trillions of shimmering bits of joy-energy, dancing in the Space of I Am.

That was fun! But it became boring again, because the One knew that it really had not split itself at all! So It created... forgetting.

Forgetting its Self, it became... separated from it's true nature! And suffering began to happen, for some aspects of The One were convinced they had lost Paradise and become separated from their Source... the One.

What to do? The One wondered? Well, I guess I will have to put a back door in the program. So the program was altered just enough to allow some of the apparently separate beings to remember... to recognize... RE-Cognize... their Identity AS the One.

Finally, The One recognized its Self as The One. How? By seeing that The One had been hiding in plain sight! In The One, what can actually be separate?

The final tweak is the realization that EVEN THE SEPARATION IS THE ONE. Playing the Cosmic Game of Hide and Seek!

Oneness Is Hiding from ItSelf – in Plain Sight

Everywhere, everywhen.

All there IS, is Oneness... and YES, even YOU, as you are, are THAT.

Period.

Full Stop.

So this book is about You as the One seeing through the game of One,

once and for good.

In other words...Allee Allee In Free!

---

the end is the beginning
this moment
has no beginning
this moment
has no end
this moment
is
from this
emanates knowingness
a movement of energy
beingness is the moment before knowingness
the eternal moment from which all emanates
        and seemingly is
vibrating soundlessly as the moving
living
me-and-world not two
until energy thinks I am and seems to separate
without thought
just this moment is
without a thought of I to label that
an I that makes itself and then more labels
just this moment is
with or without
labeling
that
eternal not begun not ended
moment is
bingo-ing
knowing-ness
energy moving
Experiencing, as I was out shopping
then I saw that experiencing gets translated
        virtually instantly into a me
        and an experience... two-ness

until now I did not notice the translation happening
so... what is the TRANSLATOR?
(it was like... IS like...
      a really good translator at the UN,
      SO fast as to almost be simultaneous!)
energy
it is all energy
loving to be
words re-present
word is not the occur-ING
      merely a report after the fact
the words are also energy...
      arising and appearing in and as
      this beginningless endless moment

I Am That Space in which the thought and the thinker,
the experience and the experiencer, ARISES...
from No Thing

I am Prior To Language

I AM not this thought that I AM

I AM Emptiness Space Awareness
Before the THOUGHT "I Am"

I am Nothing
I am that Empty and
Meaningless Space
I am Everything
I am That I am

Nothing here is true.
Nothing is Eternal.
ONLY nothing is Eternal.
From I Am to I Am, with Love!

19. A Short Version of the Story of a Me

Charlie Hayes was a "spiritual seeker" for over thirty years. He experienced much psychological suffering, and sought relief on many paths.

That search ended in 2006, thanks to the clear pointing out of the obviousness of presence of awareness, by "Sailor" Bob Adamson, Tony Parsons, John Wheeler, John Greven, Annette Nibley, and other friends.

"Caveat: I AM NOT THE STORY. The best way to describe ANY 'story of a person' would be in the words of Shakespeare: 'A tale told by an idiot, signifying nothing'."

"I have not attained some awakening or liberation or some other mythical mystical 'state.' I have nothing you don't have. I'm NOT a teacher or a 'Guru.' I simply enjoy sharing what worked for me in ending my suffering. So just consider me to be a *friend.*"

As a professional racing driver in the late fifties through the sixties, Charlie won a number of major races, which, as he says "Made me feel whole and complete. For about an hour."

"But," he notes, "Despite having wealth, fame, marvelous friends, a loving family and huge successes, there was always something missing. There was a deep fundamental sense that 'something is wrong' and 'I am not a good person.' And as my life unfolded there was a deep feeling that 'I don't belong' and that 'I am on my own in a hostile world.' Despite all the successes, there was quiet (and sometimes quite LOUD) desperation!"

Charlie became intensely active in spiritual disciplines in 1974. This was precipitated by the devastating loss of most of his possessions, his business, his home and his beloved wife, accompanied by a complete "nervous breakdown," for which he was hospitalized for a month.

After being discharged, while still on heavy medication for depression, he was exposed to the teachings of two Great Sages... Ramana Maharshi and Lao Tzu.

The sages'pointers to what is Real germinated for years, while Charlie searched through many seminars, gurus, books, tapes, meditations and practices.

He spent time in Baba Muktananda's ashrams, and worked with Werner Erhard of est fame, and spent endless hours in TM and TM Siddhi Meditation.

In 1984 he received the name "Ishan", and spent much time with Muktananda successors Swamis Nityananda and Chidvilasananda, while running a sports marketing consultancy.

In 2000 Charlie had open-heart surgery, a quadruple bypass. A new life was born, so to speak. But the suffering came on stronger than ever and Charlie thought often, "I shouldn't have had that surgery. I was about dead. I should have just let go and died."

But that was not to be.

Then in 2001 he received initiation as a Reiki Master Teacher. There was a period of real freedom, it seemed. But a piece was still missing. As the search for answers went on, in 2002 there arrived in Los Angeles a "holy man" named Sri Sri Ravi Shankar. They quickly became quite close.

The Great Enlightenment

Charlie recalls, During a period of several weeks after meeting Sri Sri, I was in love with everything and everyone. I saw NO lack or limitation and I saw that EVERYTHING was perfect, just as it is."

There was NOTHING wrong any more, "for me."

Then it began to fade, inevitably, because there was still a "me" in play that claimed this as "my" enlightenment. I got REAL depressed.

There was that deep and profound experience of oneness. But it was 'owned' by the unexamined, false, 'me.'" And soon I was back in the suffering — deeper than ever!

Since ALL experience is temporary, when it faded I was left with the same endless despair that I knew as my 'default state'. So the search began again, in earnest... I went from teacher to teacher trying to figure out what was real and who I was."

Along the way I learned, from sitting around with Wayne Liquorman and listening to tapes of his guru, Ramesh Balsekar, that this enlightenment 'I' was seeking was a MYTH. This was

VERY bad news. I could hardly stand being alive and contemplated suicide, searching the Internet for painless ways to off my body."

In 2004, I found out about Tony Parsons and listened to his CDs for hours on end, as he pointed out the raw honest truth — that no one can attain what they already are. But the one-sidedness of that message made me even MORE depressed. It was a deep resignation and existential despair — there is nothing I can do? I am doomed to suffer forever?

It was horrible.

Then in late 2004 I found John Wheeler. His writings immediately shone a laser-like light on the natural state of simple Being-Awareness. I met with John, and we e-mailed back and forth as the pointers began to sink in.

This ultimately led me to John's teacher, 'Sailor' Bob Adamson, a former student of Sri Nisargadatta Maharaj. I went off to Melbourne in September '05 and spent several days with Bob... and that was the beginning of the end."

"Since then there have been dialogues with Bob, and with John Wheeler's students John Greven and Annette Nibley. Their Natural non-conceptual being-awareness, shared and pointed to, with great love and generosity, is a gift beyond price."

In early July 2006 the search ended. "It was not that I found what I was seeking. What I found is that there is nothing to attain and no one to attain it. I Am... Being, just that. Nothing is wrong any more."

There actually never was. It was all a story!

> *Things are not what they seem,*
> *nor are they otherwise.*
> *—Lankavatara Sutra*

Part Two

From I Am to
I Am, with Love

The Dialogues

Conversations About Nothing

20. It's Just This Ever-Present Knowingness

A reader says, *Hey Charlie, just wanted to say thanks for everything on your website. :) (really enjoy the bell,(does it's job)) Great pointers from everyone and also enjoying your e-book, "Perfect Peace."*

Glad to hear it has all settled in.

Just this ever-present tacit KNOWING-nothing to do...

And doing happens...it is also clear that there is now just This... as Effortless Living. Naturally thriving and unworried about "how!"

Gangaji said that Papaji used to say that he was "lazy."
I guess that's what he meant (that he wasn't "doing" anything.)

Who knows? We'd have to have asked Papaji! But I sense he was referring to the "organism," which may very well have been "programmed" to be lazy (I know that one!) Wayne Liquorman once made the point this way – a lazy organism – appearing in This, Presence Awareness.

It seems the truth is simultaneously a verb and a noun –ever-present-knowing

That's a good one.
This is all good news, and your generous sharing will no doubt benefit others who still believe in the hopelessness of the search. You now know, you ARE the light at the "end of the tunnel." The "train" that seemed to keep running us over never was real.

21. Why Don't I See or Feel the truth?

Q: It is quite exciting for my mind to read that your search ended. I intellectually agree with every word on your web site but still I do not see and feel the truth. I wonder why it is so? Could you be kind enough to throw some light on my predicament?

A: The problem here is the I that wants to see or feel something more than the simple unadorned Presence of Being.

You know that you ARE, that you exist and are aware you exist, right?

That is IT. The big "IT"... simple presence of awareness. The knowingness that is, BEFORE the intellect labels that Is-ness with a conceptual "I Am."

This NON-conceptual I Am-ness is your true nature. That cannot be grasped by the mind. The mind, the thinking machinery, is an appearance IN this plain simple Presence Awareness.

What you are is the NO thing in which things (like the sense of being a person) appear.

You exist and you are aware. What you sought and needed to know was only ever that. You ARE That. Period. Rest as THAT.

Only a mind wants more or different. If it comes up that "I want to shed more light on this," have a look: Who is this that wants something other than what is? Where is this I or me? Without a thought IS there an I or me? Then if it is only a thought can it actually be real? Or just an imaginary entity? Like a dreamed character?

Look for the substance of that I or me and you find it absent. Then you know that what you truly *are* is Presence Awareness... just that. Nothing else. That is shining presently as your own wakeful awareness of Being.

Stay in touch if you like. Read the articles on the web site again in this light. The end of the search is at hand, right now. Just see that who has been searching does not exist and what was sought is what you always already are!

Follow-up

*Q: Is there anything I can do to firmly establish myself in the truth —
that I am awareness and not this mind/body complex?*

A: Who is NOT established? Who thinks that they are other than Awareness? You already ARE firmly established as awareness. It is only that a THOUGHT is arising in that Self-same awareness, which is then believed in as MY thought. So a thought bubbles up, "Is there anything 'I' can 'Do'..." and the I thought is taken to be "what I am." Investigate that I thought... stay with the sense of I Am and trace the I back to its Source. See that the I we believe we are that must "get established" is ONLY a thought with no independent substance or reality apart from the Presence Awareness that it arises within... and track down its source and you find it is a ghost... like a cloud, it has no substance.

*I feel my predicament at the moment is best described by your phrase
"fascination with imagination."*

A: Who is fascinated with imagination? Who is it that feels? Who is fascinated? Find out. Investigate. You know beyond doubt that you are. You cannot say, "I am not." You must BE to experience, feel, and know. Who is that Being? Look within. Look without the mind... just look for your I Am and see where it is, what is it made of; does it even really exist apart from the thought-story?

All you are fooled by is a mistaken identity. You take yourself to BE this imaginary small creature with a name and a form (body-mind.) There must be the earnest desire to be free from suffering. This core longing for what is Real will propel you to the Home you never left. You are the Guru.

As I mentioned before, do the homework. There is no way around that. The investigation into what is false must happen, as well as the seeing of what is real. What is false? The imaginary person with its foibles and failings, its stories and feelings. What is real? Presence Awareness, the simple ordinary undeniable knowing — I Am, I Exist.

Staying with the deep sense of I Amness, inquire "Who Am I?" You know that you are. Now look, what is that "I AM" that I

AM? Is it really a separate entity? If so let me locate that! Where is it? The investigation will show you that the person you persist in believing in is actually ABSENT! Then your True Nature will shine forth unimpeded by false beliefs and concepts.

I feel my attachment with ego is too strong to be just watched dispassionately.

Who is saying so? Isn't that sentence simply more thoughts arising in the Presence Awareness that you are — your simple Be-ingness? You sentence yourself to prison in thoughts! Look for the author of these sentences and you find it is a phantom! Totally UN-Real.

Again, WHO feels or says they feel this? A writer, Richard Bach, once noted, "Argue for your limitations, and sure enough, they're YOURS." Why not investigate along the lines we have discussed rather than keeping on steadfastly and stubbornly arguing for your limitations? Who is arguing? Find that one!

Therefore "complete surrender to the present moment" and acceptance of whatever life brings forth appears very difficult.

It is not difficult; it is IMPOSSIBLE – for the mind. The thinker says "this appears very difficult." WHO is the thinker?

Just buckle down and get real with the pointers: What you are is undeniable, and at the same time unimaginable. What you are not needs to be thoroughly looked into... do the investigation. The pointers are there to be used for looking, NOT intellectual understanding. In this non-duality, intellectual understanding is the booby prize! What is needed is for you to take on this Self discovery for real and in earnest.

The good thing that you said is, "It appears." YES! It appears, as the earth appears flat and the sky appears blue. We know the neither is TRUE but simply APPEARANCE. Keep that distinction in the awareness.

I wonder if you have a piece of advice for me...

See how the above pointers do. I encourage you to take on the investigation as though your very life depends on the completion of it! It is time to get real. No more ivory tower philosophy; let's get down to it and dig deep enough to find the diamond in the "Heart," your own Presence Awareness... right here, right now.

Because whether you "realize" it at the moment or not, You Are That – Being-Awareness, Loving to simply BE. Full stop!

22. Is It 'My' Awareness?

Q: You talk about Being-Awareness. It sounds like you are saying you are awareness as an individual. This confuses me, because I understand aware-ness to be impersonal, universal.

A: I'm glad you asked this! Because absolutely, this Aware-ness is NOT "my" awareness. It is simply the One Awareness that IS... One-Without-A-Second. Unicity... non-duality. Oneness.

This One-Essence is all there is in Reality. That Thou Art and That I Am, NOT two. This is impossible to grasp with the mind.

Just look right now: Do you exist? Are you aware? That aware-ness, existing-ness is the same essence that I Am and You Are and Everything Is. Oneness -- where in Oneness is there room for any separateness whatsoever?

Know thyself as that One-Awareness, Presencing as all manifestation. That is all there is.

23. Doubts And Questions?

Q: Since you kindly invited me to get my doubts and questions on the table, here goes. A "biggie" for me is a little hard to put into words, but it's something like the following: The only awareness I know is the awareness of what these eyes see, these ears think, this skin feels, and so on. Yet it appears that others are being aware of different sights, sounds, feelings, etc. I'm not aware of what you're seeing out on the West Coast, and you're not aware of what I'm seeing here on the East Coast.

A: Yes, so it APPEARS. The appearance is that there are "others seeing different things." But what is being pointed to is AWARENESS ITSELF, devoid of ANY objects. Others are objects appearing IN Awareness. "YOU" are an object appearing IN Awareness. This is directly and undeniably known, but NOT by the mind. THAT, Presence Awareness, is NOT an Object and as such is unimaginable.

It also appears that the earth is flat. Intelligence knows it is not. Knowing that does not change the appearance... it still looks as though you'll fall off the edge if you sail too far out. The illusion... imagination... is that *you see* as a separate entity and what you see and what others see is different. That's the play! But in fact, the brute knowingness that you exist... AS awareness of presence... IS what is, always before any objects are defined by the mind. One important point here: The answer is NOT in the mind!

Now let's check our premises: The premise, or assumption in the background, in the question is that there is a you and a me. That "I" am seeing something on the "West Coast" DIFFERENT from what "You" see on the "East Coast!" This is very simply imagination... "You" and "I" and objects seen are concepts appearing ON the cinema screen of pure NON-Conceptual Awareness. This fixation on an identity that sees objects IS what needs to be seen as false... the flat earth. Awareness-Presence can be said to be the pure Non-Conceptual "I AM" BEFORE the mind translates that Space-Like Awareness into the THOUGHT "I am"... which gives rise to "Others Are."

So in what sense is there oneness, a single undivided Presence Awareness in which all things appear, if different body-minds are having different "awareness" experiences?

In the sense that awareness ITSELF... that which is Seeing, Hearing, Knowing, is what is being pointed to. For you to be aware of what you see and hear and feel, AWARENESS must be there first... not awareness OF objects; just blank ordinary Isness, Being, Awareness as ITSELF. Imagining, and then focusing on, objects OF awareness, is the job of the mind, which divides up awareness and objects of awareness. The mind is the dividing energy that seems to create all the diverse objects and blur the distinction between awareness-as-itself and objects appearing on that, like images on a cinema screen.

Or ... is there only "this," what is being experienced right now, without reference to a "me" or to "others"?

Bingo!

I recently read a quotation of Huang Po that has been bugging/haunting me ever since: "The perceived does not perceive." Does this mean there are no "others" -- the folks who appear in this Presence Awareness -- who are perceiving something different from what is being perceived here?

Good enough, as a concept. But remember that these concepts are pointers only. Many "spiritual people" have great collections of "enlightened concepts" which become another burden for the "entity." Look where they point; then drop them ALL.
In your own direct experience: Are there others apart from an appearance in awareness? See the flat earth nature of that. And yes, the perceived does not perceive and the perceiver CANNOT perceive itself. The Perceiver... Awareness, Presence... is what you ARE. The eye cannot see itself... the One cannot see itself. It IS the see-ING – Livingness – ALIVENESS ITSELF. FULL STOP. You cannot "see" your True Nature... you ARE your True Nature. THIS is why we say, your search is futile; you already ARE That which has been sought. The best way to keep from knowing what you are

is to seek to know what you are. That Thou Art – Presence Awareness. Just That.

As the Tibetans point out: What you already always ARE is Non-Conceptual, Self-Shining, Ever Fresh Presence Awareness... just this and nothing else.

Right now, right here, you ARE. THAT is all that has been sought. Right now and right here, IS there ANY separate entity, in direct experience? Look for a separate "me" and you must see it is totally absent. Then you are no longer fooled by appearance, like you no longer believe the earth is flat. Drop the belief in the entity, see that you are Presence Awareness.

Any problem seeing right now that awareness is present, before any sense of time, space, object, and other, arises?

Grok these concepts and then toss 'em out!

Keep me posted... let's get this nailed down once and for good.

24. This Knowing Is NON-Conceptual

Q: Many like to speak in absolutes, but The Upanishads suggest that "He who thinks he knows It not, knows It. He who thinks he knows It, knows It not."

A: The knowing is NON-Conceptual. One who thinks he knows, knows not, because there is a thinker-knower.

That which we are... Presence Awareness... is known as simply being aware of existing... not as a concept. That is NON-conceptual.

You know that you exist and are aware without a thought. Impossible for the mind to grasp... so don't look there... the answer is NOT in the mind, or books, or anywhere other than in your own direct Awareness of Being.

Forget the scriptures. They are all dry lifeless concepts!

You exist and you are aware.

THAT alone is beyond doubt. That is Present Moment Aliveness... All else is dust. What you sought and needed to know was only ever this. You ARE That. Period.

Who is thinking that they do not see That? Who thinks there is more than That?

THAT is Home.

25. Who Is Bipolar and Depressed?

Q: Let me ask you. Do you think your bi-polar helped you ultimately with your realization or do you think you would have ever if you hadn't cured your bi-polar first?

A: It's apples and oranges, David... it really does not matter what the manifestation "is." Just seeing the dream as a dream; the character as seen as a dreamed character. NOTHING touches or obscures the simple, ordinary Presence Awareness.

Ask yourself: Do I Exist? Am I aware? There is never a time when that Being is NOT... before time, before space, before depression, before all that appears, that I Am Existence always IS... just see that THAT is what we are, and then the search is over.

Who Is Depressed?

WHO is depressed? WHO is bi-polar? Even knowing you are human arises IN the I Am awareness. You are the knower, not the known objects. This is what the sages are pointing to when they suggest, "stay with the I Am." If you have your stand in what changes you will continue to suffer! Shift your identity to "I Am." The knowing-Knower of all that is known never changes. Nothing that changes can be real. Only THAT Awareness-Being is real!

Before consciousness IS, YOU EXIST. That Thou Art. Full stop!

Handling the machinery of the body-mind with medicine is no different than giving it food that works. Some foods work for the body mind called David and some don't. Experimenting is fine. Just don't confuse "peace of mind" or it's opposite with the Being-ness, the I Am.

The Beloved is sitting right there on your shoulder beckoning right now: "I'm here, David. Just turn around, and see Me. I Love you. I AM you."

PS: "I" did NOT "cure" "my" bipolar. The assumptions in that line are at the very root core of suffering. You assume there is a separate "Charlie." Then you assume there is such a "thing" as "bipolar." All of these labels have no reality apart from the awareness

they arise within, as language. IT'S ALL A STORY! There is no person, no depression, no happiness, no problem, no solution, no
dream, and no dreamer; all there is, IS what IS, as IT IS. Here and
now.

26. Aaahhh

Ah !!!!
It's good being home.
Love,
Ruth
Xoxoxoxo

Yes! Welcome to the Home you never left!

27. I Cannot Think My Way Out of Suffering

Q: I've found, Charlie, that I cannot think myself out of suffering. Yet I've also experienced the Hellish torture of accepting parts of myself (or perhaps, what I believe to be myself on a level that carries far more energy than anything I can consciously muster or change) that I've attempted to deny and come out on the other side in peace and acceptance.

A: You are quite right, "you" cannot think yourself out of suffering:

One: There is NO "you!" So "you" will never know peace and acceptance. This is NOT a matter of some "personal" attainment. There is no you! Peace and acceptance is natural when "you" are ABSENT.

Two: You, as your true nature, are ALREADY outside of suffering. There is nowhere to go and no one to go there!

Looking in the mind will NEVER work. Nor will any practice. All practices are for "you" and there simply isn't one. Practices reinforce the idea of being a separate entity that must get somewhere that it isn't.

It sounds like there is a basic misunderstanding about what has been pointed to.

Bottom line: Presence Awareness is NOT conceptual, not a mental construct. THAT is what you are. Non-conceptual, ever fresh, self-shining Presence Awareness, just this and NOTHING ELSE.

Consider this and do not reject until there is a non-conceptual seeing! And, there is seeing, by no one, that the separate entity called "you" is a phantom! That phantom, that ghost, is merely a thought story! All imagination... and only imagination. All that troubles you is your own imagination!

What the ancients and the sages refer to as our REAL Self is Just This: You exist and you are aware. What was sought was only ever this. Stop right now and look: Are you present and aware? Even if the mind says no, you must be aware to claim unawareness!

Realize that all you ever sought and needed to know is this. There is no mystery to this: You are, simply, Presence Awareness, being, timeless and undeniable. Just that. Where does That begin or end? When is That NOT? That Never Changes... and That, Thou Art.

Now, look for a separate "individual" called "yourself" and you find it completely absent. There is no entity apart from what you are... Non-Dual Presence Awareness... simply Being.

The direct seeing of this is the Peace that surpasses understanding. This is The Home you never left.

A little looking with the Intelligence-energy and seeing can happen. It is NOT a mystery!

Let me know how it goes.

28. Worn Out By Demands Of The World

Q: It's hard to stay focused on Enlightenment. On the other hand, the masters say there is no enlightenment because I am already enlightened, soooooooo perhaps it's much ado about nothing. Why bother? :-) Did you "do" anything particular, besides stay with the sense I AM, never wavering? I find that hard to do. Is it necessary?

A: What works is, stick with the basics. You are aware that you exist, right? No one can deny his or her own beingness. You are. THAT is beyond doubt or argument. No need to "stay with the I Am." Who would do that? And as you already ARE why a need to "stay with" that? Try to escape from being. Seeing. Hearing. Heart beating. Thoughts arising and subsiding. All happening presently, and that simple knowing that you exist and are aware is what seekers seek... never seeing that they already ARE what they seek.

Then the other side of this non-dual coin is, where is any separate entity called me or you?

I'm terribly worn out with the demands of this world and could use whatever there is to stop all the worry and anxiety.

What is called for here is looking (NOT thinking about) at the nature of the "person" who is suffering with worry and anxiety. Who is anxious? Who is worried? Understand that the only thing that can trouble you is you own imagination. Where is there a problem unless you think about it? And WHO is the thinker?

The investigation naturally happens when there is suffering and a desire arises to find and root out the source of that suffering, which turns out to be nothing more complex that an unexamined belief in a phantom, a self-image, all constructed on top of the thought "I"... and the THOUGHT "I" is not the I of Consciousness-awareness. The thought is a representation, a translation by the thought-machine, of the pure I Consciousness, the simple, ordinary, Presence Awareness that you are. This awareness is self-shining, NON-conceptual beingness.

There is a huge paradox in all this. In truth there is no person. It is not that there is nothing to be done, it is that there IS no one to do or not do anything. But so long as we do not live in and as that Understanding, then looking can happen. There is no one; AND so long as it seems there is someone, the investigation happens. Once the gateless gate has been passed, then it is seen, by no one, that there never was a dream or a separate character or any investigation. Then life flows simply and effortlessly... for no one. All is just happening in this that you are... Awareness-Presence.

But the bottom line is, the seeing and knowing of this is NON-conceptual. It is closer than your breath.

The answer is NOT in the mind or in books or in Satsang or anywhere but right where you are. Wherever you go there YOU are as this presence of awareness.

So the basics of this boil down to:

Awareness is present; I am that.

The person is absent, I am not that.

This awareness is obviously present at all times. It is non-conceptual, just the natural knowing of your actual ever present BEING.

Stay in touch as the spirit moves. Get all the doubts and questions out to examine. Freedom is your true nature; suffering is NOT necessary.

What really fascinates me is considering the waking world to be of the same substance as the dream world. It may help "me" when I consider that everything, including this body and even all these thoughts and worries is just a mental construct, just like a dream. Not important. But just a fun show to watch. Of course "most" all of the characters in this waking world consider everything they do very important. It is nice to know that there are a few characters in the waking dream that know this is just a dream and that all this striving and struggling is for naught.

Keep looking: Where is the "me" that considers "the waking world to be of the same substance as the dream world"? What is its nature? Does it even exist apart from a thought story that arises in the Presence Awareness that you are? Does it have any substance or independent existence apart from awareness? Where is this "me" located? Is it in the body? Where? Which cell is "you?" all the cells are replaced every seven years. So where is this you residing? Is it in the "mind?" All the mind is, is thoughts... movements of energy forming into letters-words all related to a (false) reference point.

Where is any person apart from thought, imagination? Dig deep.

It is NOT that "striving and struggling are for naught." All sense of striving and struggling is the hallmark of a belief in a separate entity, a "me," which on sufficient investigation is found to be completely NON-existent!

Find the "me" to be absent and life becomes naturally effortless, as a being lived. The doer is gone, and all there is, is what is... moment-by-moment, in perfect freedom. Take a good look with these pointers. Let me know how it goes, OK?

29. What Is the "I" That Says, "I See?"

Q: I can "see" the "story of me" taking place within me all the time. But at the same time I also feel the past conditioning of mind continues to give momentum to this "I" story and does not allow it to disappear or to fall apart.

A: Just notice that there is still an "I" that "sees the story of me"... investigate, who or what IS that "I" that says, "I see?" Seeing is happening. Seeing trees, seeing a "me-story", seeing cars, seeing marks on a screen forming words and concepts which mind interprets. There is NO "I" in Seeing. The I thought comes later, a nanosecond after the appearance of whatever is arising. "You" are NOT needed for life to be lived through that body-mind organism!

Seeing your true nature as Presence Awareness is one side of this non-dual coin. The other is seeing that the "I" or "me" is FALSE. This can only happen through looking in the space of your own non-dual awareness and seeing that this vaunted "I" is only a thought appearing in the empty sky-like awareness that you are. Then the story is seen AS just a story with no power to disturb that pure awareness. What power does a thought have? None. It is the unfinished investigation into whether or not thoughts are real that keeps the mind fixated on the phantom of the opera, the totally false self-center, "Me, myself and I"... !

Just see the false AS false, then the energy of belief no longer goes into that story. Then you realize in your own space that nothing can trouble you except your own imagination.

You had mentioned in one of your messages to me that I should do the homework first in order to know the truth. Could you kindly elaborate what homework needs to be done?

Just this gentle persistent looking to see: What is True is Presence Awareness. What is false is this idea of there being any separate entity whatsoever. The thought "I Am" is NOT the true I Am of Being-Awareness. Seeing this takes just a willingness to look without the mind; the answer is NOT in the mind.

Look within yourself right now:

Is there a separate entity?

Where is it?

What is it made of?

Looking in this way you realize that this ego-entity is utterly absent. There never has been an entity! Don't stop till you see beyond doubt that this "entity" is a chimera, a phantom, like a dream character, that never was, as is seen on waking from the sleep dream.

Consider these pointers, look into the space, and see what you see... and keep me posted!

30. Who feels finished and at peace?

A friend writes, Papaji used to say: "call off the search." After Sailor Bob's uncompromising message, I seem to be doing just that. I feel finished and feel at peace just the way things are NOW.

There is a red flag in this as it is seen and felt here. If "you" feel finished and at peace, you can absolutely count on that feeling going away! These cosmic experiences of peace and completion are temporary. Just thought-feeling stories in a mind that will NEVER know its Source.

Are you present? Aware? Do you exist? That non-conceptual simplicity of Being-Awareness is what you sought, what you are. ANY experience can come and go IN that, whether you feel like crap or feel great. It makes NO difference what the content of Awareness is... anything can arise in That. If you have your stand in experiences you are in for a crash, dear friend. Take on that what you are IS NON conceptual Isness, Beingness, the No Thing in which all that is arises. Then see without thought that this No Thing is Energy, Intelligence, Aliveness itself, not a thing, but EVERY thing.

The belief in an individual entity that has "made it at long last" will trip you up sooner or later. An incomplete investigation leaves subtle remnants of this belief in a separate "me" or "I" and MUST be completely seen through; otherwise you are left with an inauthentic and paltry sense of peace, while ignoring the immensity of the Freedom of your Natural State.

Don't settle for this. Keep looking until you are absolutely certain that there is NO person in the machine.

31. All That Is, Just IS, AS It Is, Is NOT a "Feeling"

Been feeling lately that everything is what it is, neither good nor bad.

That is a powerful insight. However a word of caution... the brute fact that all that is, just IS, AS it is, is NOT a feeling. It is simply what's so, before the mind/emotions take over and co-opt That into a sense-feeling. Nevertheless, that is a great sign!

Only imagination makes it good or bad.

Exactly! As Nisargadatta said, the ONLY thing that can trouble you is your own imagination. It's good to ask here, WHOSE imagination? Do "I" author that thought story? Who am I? Whose thoughts are they? Mine? Who is the "me" referred to by the thought "me?" The always already response of the mind? "I Am." Then in looking at that thought "I Am" and effortlessly rejecting all appendages TO that thought, the Source of the THOUGHT "I Am" reveals its Self to its Self... in a manner of speaking (look where the concept points, NOT at the concept itself!)

Thinking can be a debilitating disease... I just about got an ulcer worrying about the future the other day... what if I don't pass this math test? What if I don't pass this math class... OMG...

And there you have it: The disease of the mind. Applying the same inquiry, into the one who thinks... who IS that!?... then it can be seen that all these thoughts simply show up... uninvited. And for whom do they show up? "Me." Okay, who is that "me?" Is it real? Or simply another thought arising unbidden!?

Turning the focus back to the "I Am" (represented in the mind by the *thought* "I Am") and refusing the additional subjective add-ons (I am a student, I have "my" math test, I am a person, I am not good enough, I am small and limited, I am afraid) cuts the cord on the suffering. It's worth some work! Then the Pure Subject shines brightly (as it always already does anyhow) and it is seen, by no "person," Aha! I AM That Light. I am NOT the object called "me"... and never was.

That's it. Therein is the clear and present Seeing that there is no "me" and never was. And nothing is "wrong" any more. If a thought of "wrongness" arises, when the "me-myself-I" is seen to ALSO merely be a thought, the idea of "something wrong" has nothing to attach to and the illusory fixation (that never actually was) "ends," as the energy of belief can no longer attach to that which is now seen to be unreal. Then the thought just dissipates like a cloud in the bright light of the ever-present empty sky. And that Light is Home... the Home you never really left.

Then the game of hide and seek that Self has played with its Self is over and done.

Allee Allee In Free!

Here is a quote that may resonate for you given what you are sharing currently:

"Give up all questions except one: 'Who Am I?' After all, the only fact you can be sure of is that you ARE. The 'I Am' is certain. The 'I am this' is not."

    –Sri Nisargadatta Maharaj, *I Am That*

The inquiry leaves you squarely in the lap of the undeniable "I AM" that you are... the space-like Presence Awareness represented in the mind by the thought "I Am." Then abiding AS that I Am-ness is effortless and sublime.

Consider:

The Raw Crispness of Now

Look to the root, before thought arises
What is the essence of that?
That is not apart from this,
but is what supports and contains it
  – Burt Jurgens, Beyond Description

As "Burt" knows full well, this Now is actually yet another concept, and in actuality there is NO Now.

Now presupposes some "time" (past, or future) OTHER than Now. Impossible as all there is, is Not Now.

As the sage Seng T'san noted, the great way is timeless and formless: "The great way is beyond language. In it there is no yesterday, NO tomorrow, *No today.*"

Timeless Being, Absolute Presence Awareness, arising as Consciousness and its content, manifests as all that is... Consciousness-Totality arising as the impossibly immense appearance IN that Absolute.

Sounds like two things... but only to "a mind." Reality is simply Not Two.

Being. Just That.

> *The moment you know your real being, you are afraid of nothing. Death gives freedom and power. To be free in the world, you must die to the world. Then the universe is your own, it becomes your body, an expression and a tool. The happiness of being absolutely free is **beyond description**.*
> —Sri Nisargadatta Maharaj

32. Don't We Need to Act to Avoid Ending Up Broke?

Russell writes, *"It's nice to hear that the search has finally ended for you. What a ride it was!!, wasn't it? To go full circle, great cosmic joke. Oneness playing the game of hide and seek. Well, game over."*

Yep. The great Cosmic Roller Coaster.

I just finished reading your book and there certainly are many great pointers in it that point to our true nature (Oneness). I do however have a question — on page 38, you stated: All 'my worries'...about money, health, ending up homeless unless I find work, getting old, feeling insecure and vulnerable and so alone... only arise in thinking... and as "Sailor" Bob notes... "What's wrong with Right now... unless you think about it?" I agree that it does arise only in thinking as a thought but even though thoughts aren't real and appear only in our imagination, don't we still need to act on these thoughts or else we will end up homeless, broke, etc...."

The assumption in the background of your question (which is a very good one) is, there IS a "me" ("WE need to act") that must "decide" to act and then act. I remind you that as the Buddha declared, "Actions happen, deeds are done, but there is NO individual doer thereof." That "me"... the phantom "individual"... is but another THOUGHT arising in awareness... here and now. ALL is appearing in that awareness that we are... and the thought "I am a person who must act to survive" IS suffering!

There well may be actions that happen (spontaneously, as everything happens spontaneously) that result in the bills being paid and homelessness averted. BUT NO ONE DOES THEM. This is the crucial pointer... ALL suffering is only for the imaginary person! The pointer is, there is nothing wrong unless thinking is taken to be real by the so-called individual... which has no independent existence or reality apart from a movement of energy in awareness. Without the belief in the fixating "entity" there is NO problem, no solution, no past, no future, no present. It is all simply a thought-feeling storm arising presently IN and AS an aspect OF Awareness-Presence.

But don't BELIEVE this crap either! Look for any separate "person" where you are, in the simple ordinary awareness that you are, and you find it is absent. Then the question evaporates, along with the questioner... and THAT is HOME... Being, the home you never really left.

Also, Nisargadatta noted that "nothing can trouble you but your own imagination." But again I say, don't we live in our imagination even though I am fully aware that I do not exist as an entity. Real or not real makes no difference when these thoughts arise and action must be taken. This does not touch Awareness, our true nature , but we will have a bad dream if not acted on. Confusion is appearing at this moment.

Again, WHO is this "we" or "me" that "lives in imagination?" The pointer is that the "me" ITSELF IS imagination! The confusion arises as a *product* of that "mistaken identity ONLY."

Look deeply for this ME... Who am I? What is real? Only what NEVER changes can be the Real. What is It that never changes? The I thought comes and goes... therefore it cannot be what is Real. Apart from awareness itself, do I have any real independent existence as a "me" apart from pure Awareness its Self?

When the investigation is still incomplete, there are vestiges of belief in a separate entity... and that entity appears to suffer, until rooted out at the core. Keep looking, with affection for the TRUE "I Am." Stay with the sense of the pure "I Am" that you know as your own Presence of simply Being, and reject any and all "add-ons" such as "I am Russell. I am the one who must act to avoid homelessness, etc."

You will know the investigation is done when there is no "you" apart from Beingness to "know" that! Then it is seen, there never was a "seeker" or a "person" in Reality. Nothing ever happened!

As the dream at night is seen to be false on awakening to the waking state, the waking state is seen to be false on investigation and THAT is "game over." The Roller Coaster has come to a Full Stop and there is a sigh of relief, maybe a thought "That was a wild ride!" and then... Nothing. No Thing. Then, the unreal is simply no longer taken to be the Real. Full Stop. I am speaking from direct experience, to the I Am that you actually ARE. You are NOT what thinks "you" into seeming existence!

Where Is the Phantom of My Opera?

There is no actual "ghost in the machine." Find out! Keep the inquiry alive until there is no one to inquire. And keep me posted. Let's get this matter of the nattering "me" resolved once and for good... right here, right now.

The Light shining before the mind-imagination IS that which allows the reading of this, the seeing, the hearing, the knowing of Existence its Self. THAT is what you are. Don't refuse to be what you are!

To paraphrase the Zen master Bankei, EVERYTHING is naturally and effortlessly resolved in the Unborn. Don't trade the Unborn (Presence Awareness) for thoughts.

What'll Happen to MEeeee?

Going broke and being homeless may happen. A new source of income may happen and homelessness is averted. The body-mind organism my disintegrate and expire before money runs out. ANYTHING can happen in the Dream of this "matrix" we call "my life." We are along for the ride, until there is no one and the ride is seen for what it is... the Cosmic Dance, the Dream of the "Individual."

The little "me" can NEVER KNOW what is next. Do you even know what your next thought will be? Abiding as not knowing is another description for Being, Awareness-Presence. ALL "knowing" is ignorance (ignoring our True Nature as the Light of Awareness.)

Here is another Pointer... in the interest of Absolute Clarity in the Seeing of This As It Is...

You wrote, "*I get it.*"

Now, take the I that "got it" out of the road. Then take the "It" out. Then the "Get." What's left? That, Thou Art.Full Stop!

33. Forms and the Formlessness Are Not Two

Follow-Up from Russell: *Thanks for replying to my email. If I understand correctly, what you are saying is that what I am is Presence Awareness, just that and nothing else. All add-ons are thought forms appearing as real.*

Right on.

What appears on the face of Awareness is just appearances only and is not to be taken for as real.

The appearances are aspects OF Presence Awareness and not separate from That. So the appearances are REAL in that they ARE Presence Awareness, appearing AS forms. The forms and the formless are Not Two.

What appears is what is happening in the now and no ownership by the phantom "me" should grasp it as real.

Watch out for the old "should" word. Only an entity... the phantom... has any concern for shoulds or should nots... those concepts are pinned onto a belief in time. It is the mind stepping back into the game... just see that for what it is... the Play of Presence Awareness. Take away the should and all that follows and THAT, Oneness, is clear, and the phantom "me" is then seen for what it is... nothing but a movement of the Energy-Intelligence that consists IN and AS Awareness Herself. (So to speak! There is such deep Love in That.)

So, if for example, going broke or being homeless is appearing, then acceptance of what is happening is really the only choice we truly have.

What is this we? Where is there any "one" called "me" or "we" to choose? The whole idea of choice and chooser is nothing but thought arising presently in the Empty Sky of Presence Awareness. It is just a chain reaction of thoughts – moving energy – arising, which have no real substance... unless the energy of that core belief in the "I" goes into them, and unconsciously they are taken on board as "my" thoughts, "my" circumstances, "my" acceptance.

In TRUE acceptance there is NO acceptor. No doer, no author. There is NO choice, no chooser... all that happens is, thought forms arise that are pinned squarely onto that core belief in a separate entity... the Phantom of "My Opera." Mistaken identity... that is all that is! It is just a misunderstanding that investigation proves false.

Now as I write this, a question arises. If for example, I do go broke and become homeless, then that is what is happening...

Yes. And there may be thoughts of acceptance or not and THAT is what is happening. But all this speculation is more mind stuff! Just see that all that is happening right NOW is thought stories, appearing presently – then taken on board and "worried about." The worrying is only due to an incomplete investigation: "Who is worried? Me. Who is THAT? Where is it? What is the Source of this Me-Myself-I taken on board as real and substantial?" Ask until "you" drop! "Who AM I? I know I AM. That is obvious and undeniable." Yet WHAT that IS the mind CANNOT grasp! Stop looking for answers in the mind; do the inquiry as long as there is ANY vestige of belief in a separate "do-er" remaining. "Who Am I? Who Thinks? Who Chooses? Who? Who?"

The only "true" concept the mind can deliver is "I Am." And the THOUGHT I Am is NOT the actual I AM of pure Awareness, Being... that knowingness that you are, "I AM," is NEVER absent. Stay with that knowingness!

It is all very simple. Instead of seeing things as imagined, learn to see them as they really ARE. When you can see everything as it is, you will also see yourself as you are. It is like cleansing a mirror. The same mirror that shows you the world as it is, will also show you your own face. The thought "I Am" is the polishing cloth. Use it.

−Sri Nisargadatta Maharaj

As long as there is ANY sense of a "Russell" there, dwell on the thought I Am and trace it back to its Source. The thought will evaporate other thoughts, and will also disappear. What will be left is your Original Face... empty and at the same time gloriously full. True Nature... Home.

The phantom "I" suffers but if it does not exist then is it Oneness that is experiencing suffering?

Oneness IS the experience-ING. In That... True Self... there is NO false triad of Experience/experiencer/process of experience. Just the Livingness of the experiencing. BUT: Oneness does NOT "experience suffering." THAT is a solid block of Pure Reality, Being-Awareness.

As they say, water cannot wet That, fire cannot burn That, a sword cannot cut That. That, what you actually are, is invincible, and unimaginable. The answer is NOT in the thinker-mind.

So, in a way, suffering is happening at this moment but to no one? Is this correct?

Again, Oneness does NOT "experience suffering." As a concept, this is close... but keep the distinction clear and present... that NO concept is the ACTUAL. The concept, the word, the thought of "fire" will NOT burn your hand no matter how loud you shout it.

Suffering is rooted in the belief "I am the body." Aren't ALL your worry thoughts related to a self-centered identification of your "self as an object" (a body or a mind?) You are NOT an object! You are the Light that illumines ALL objects, like the projector light illumines the transparent pictures on the film and seems to make them real on the screen... You ARE the Light. Just That and nothing else.

It is a ONLY belief in a "me" that can cause suffering. That IS the root cause of suffering. It is a better pointer to say, "Pain can arise... for no one." But suffering is totally false when the fake "me" is exposed and rooted up once and for good!

Trying to get to the bottom of this.

Who is trying? Find out.

I LOVE your earnestness. Keep at it... trace that Source of ALL thoughts, and see the I as ONLY a thought once and for good.

Then there is the seeing that all is appearance, In That Oneness and as an ASPECT of That.

Here, IT is especially noticed as THAT called "Charlie" is out and about, as today it was off to the car dealer, the doctor's office, the drug store, the grocery shop and the office supply place.

I see (more accurately said as "it is seen") that there are all these separately appearing organisms and other forms but there is nothing and no one in them!

If it weren't so natural the mind would grab on and call it amazing.

34. Using Mind to Free Mind? Sounds Oxymoronic!

Q: It looks like thought is really the enemy. So practices are a waste of time... But asking myself "Who am I?" as you and Ramana and Nisargadatta suggest still uses the mind. Using the mind to be free of the mind? Wouldn't it be better to just be aware of awareness? I know that sounds like meditation though, which is just another practice... ha!

This is an excellent question. And, I ask you to look, "Who is asking the question?"

Thoughts are NOT "the enemy." They are simply movements in Awareness of "Energy-Intelligence"... that which keeps the stars apart.

And. all these thoughts arising about "to meditate or not, isn't inquiry using the mind, etc." arise right in that Presence Awareness-Being-ness that is your True Nature. So simply see without the seer! That it is ALL simply arising.

The pointer is looking, NOT "thinking about." This natural stateless state can never be grasped by the dualistic thinker-mind! Simply looking, noticing, leads to the natural seeing that awareness is primary and the only true Reality.

Meditation, self inquiry, and being aware of awareness arise. But ask yourself, "Who is aware of Awareness?" Find that one... if "you" can!

The answer is not in the mind. Yet, the suffering, and subsequent seeking, arises IN the so-called mind (mind is just another thought, there actually IS no "mind!") But see, the mind cannot "know awareness" because it is an OBJECT arising IN the Light of Pure Awareness! So where IS the answer? No where. Everywhere. Full Stop.

The idea of a mind freeing itself is of course totally ignorance, as you are seeing. I love your question because it indicates real, rigorous looking over there where awareness calls itself "you" and my sense of it is that a wee bit more non-conceptual looking, embracing the totally PARADOXICAL nature of all this, and it will be seen by no one that there never WAS a seeker, a questioner, or a question... just empty thoughts arising and disappearing again like insubstantial clouds in the brilliant light of the sky.

Now, Here, all that there actually is, is what you are, that which never changes, Being... just that.

And That is That!

Follow-Up

Yeah, I get it. Ask "Who am I?" – then actually look and see. Looking and seeing is really very easy. After dismissing the world, the body, and thought as who I am, there isn't anything left. :-) And there never WAS any "entity"... No Thing is left, and then even THAT goes! If there is a sense of a me lingering, "I" am aware of that also....so once again, there is nothing conceptual left which could be me.

Bingo!

Just need to post that up on the wall in big letters, ha.
Thanks for replying.

No need to "post on the wall." The Knowing is clear, and any "wanting to hang on" to a concept (that arises ONLY Presently!) can (seemingly) dilute the clarity that is so evident in your message.

As Ramana pointed out, once the thorn (concept) has been used to remove the embedded thorn (erroneous concept of the I thought) then both thorns are tossed out. Otherwise you end up carrying a big bag of rocks (concepts) around and having to fish through them for a memory of an insight! That is death.

Just notice the desire that arises as thoughts of wanting to remember or hold onto an idea is simply the mind kicking back into gear and attempting to usurp the clear Understanding and make it into a "personal attainment."

My sense is that you see all this and in a way this is preaching to the choir! But it just bubbled up to be said.

35. Still Suffering Despite 'Understanding'

Gary F. writes, I read parts of "From I Am To I Am with Love" and was knocked out by the clarity and the confidence with which you have written it.

My interest in writing the book — although in truth the thing wrote itself! — is that it be helpful to those who are still (seemingly) embedded in the belief in a "me" that suffers. So far that seems to be the case.

It really does!

It sounds like there are no further sufferings, doubts or questions there... true?

I don't have any questions, and there is really nothing to doubt, but I can no longer claim (as I have been doing for the past year or so, mostly to myself) that I don't suffer any more.

Who is the "I" that is ever claiming or no longer claiming ANYTHING? Who is the owner? Who is the "myself?" Isn't all that just mind-chatter? Isn't the knowingness always there, that you ARE? No one can deny their own already always ever present knowingness... that I Am. THAT is the ONLY true thought... and ultimately it IS seen that the THOUGHT "I Am" is not the ACTU-AL "I Am" of Pure unalloyed ever-fresh Presence Awareness, the ONLY unchanging Reality. The word fire won't burn your hand.

All the thoughts in the universe cannot ever obliterate that knowingness. It is too simple for the mind to grasp... so I respect-fully suggest, quit looking there.

Your e-mail indicates that there is still a solid belief in an entity called Gary! If there is such a separate entity, pull it out and look at it!

The discipline to inquire is naturally born of suffering. Go full out asking, "Who Am I"... as thoughts of this and that arise, have a fresh look... "To whom do these thoughts and feelings (and pains) occur? To Me? Who is that Me? Where is it? What is its Source?"

Track THAT down once and for good and it evaporates — simply because all that "I-Myself-Me-Mine" complex is, is insubstantial thoughts that cannot even appear unless the Awareness of Being is there (Here.) And in actual fact, as you pointed out, they never WERE real!

Last week I was in excruciating pain and I really saw how identified I STILL am, even after repeating about a 1000 times, "I am not the body...I am not the body....I am not the body..", etc. and trying to convince myself (unsuccessfully) that I was only experiencing PAIN and that I wasn't really SUFFERING.

This SEEING is NOT a matter of the mind being convinced. Or not. Pain is pain and as such is not really an issue until thinking kicks in (a nanosecond late, by the way) and claims to OWN the pain... "I hurt and I should NOT hurt and I want what is to NOT be as it is." It's all just thoughts. Who is thinking? Who owns the pain? Only the still believed-in "I" thought. Just Mistaken Identity. Root it OUT.

There has been great pain here, recently, from a chronic back problem. But there is no suffering, because the one who can suffer has been thoroughly investigated over the year and a half plus since the first meeting with John Wheeler. And seen to be completely nonexistent. Pure Awareness, appearing as Consciousness and all the content of Consciousness, the I Am, is all that is actually real. That NEVER changes. Find THAT. Be still. Be.

Assertions, declarations, and affirmations are simply more thoughts. Instead of repeating with the thinker-mind, "I am not the body," ask WHO is saying that? Who is making this claim? That will take you back to the core concept "I Am." Stay with that I Am — the undeniable sense of knowingness that you always exist — and trace that "I" thought back to Source.

This inquiring into the truth or falseness of the separate "I" will unconceal the actual NON-conceptual I Am-Ness once and for good. Once the false is SEEN as false there is simply no way the energy of belief can go into it any more. Then you see clearly that there is no seer, simply the seeing.

I had to confess I was not quite the liberated comedian I talked myself into believing that I was.

Thanks for that honesty! It is refreshing. Gary, we have all gone through that one. There are good examples in James Braha's book, <u>Living Reality</u>.

A lot of that sort of delusion was experienced here! The good news is, you have seen through that illusion, and now you can get real with the pointers: What you ARE, said in words which cannot actually express what is, IS... Self-Shining, Ever-Fresh, Non-Conceptual, Presence Awareness, just this and Nothing else. No thing.

Rather than buy into the mind-feeling machinery that claims any attainment OR any "LACK" simply *STOP at I Am. Dwell AS That.*

STOP going along with the habitual habit patterns in thinking. Question every single thought with the query... "Who is thinking? Who is asking the questions? Who is claiming to know OR not know anything?" If you look right now do you even know what the next arising thought will be? Focus on the I AM, Awareness, just that.

Now INTELLECTUALLY I know that I am No Thing, nor could EVER be, except through false identification plus a few vain imaginings... and yet... and yet...

Delete the word intellectually and what is left? "I know that I am No Thing."

Period. Stop.

Add nothing to that No thing.

Strike the "and yet"... that's simply the thinker... the false "I"... trying its level best to keep its phantom nature by being believed in and added on to. That can only survive through lack of inquiry! That is very good news. So buckle down and keep looking, my friend. Take the one who says, "I know I am no thing" out of the road.

That No Thing, Thou Art. That No Thing, I Am. That No Thing is all that IS. No Thing... expressing as the arising and disappearing of Every thing.

There is so much Love in That. Keep after that "I" thought until it evaporates once and for good! See the True as True (I AM) and see the false as false (The imaginary me-myself-and-I.)

36. Stay With Non-Conceptual I-Am-Ness

Follow-Up from Gary F.: *Charlie, I just read your response....GREAT stuff!!! have to re-read it a few times to digest it ALL...*

That is a good plan!

I'm finding a lot LOVE in your responses to everyone and that is the REAL sign that you are coming from the space of the REAL.

It takes One to "know" One. Unconditional Absolute Love ultimately recognizes (RE-cognizes) its own Self. Then that too disappears into the sublime Silence of The Absolute, out of which Consciousness arises and all the appearances appear.

I'm getting a lot from our dialogues too, now that I realize I have over-estimated my own "realization"... how easy it is to be deceived into thinking that "I am Enlightened"... I am Nothing, so there's no thing or no one to Enlightened...

Exactly. No Thing. And "mind," being an object appearing in Awareness-Presence, can NEVER grasp No Thing.

Now drop even THAT concept. What is left? NON-conceptual Nothing... and Everything... paradoxically, Not Two. There is only That.

I'm really feeling this...

"THIS" is NOT a FEELING. That is a crucial pointer... simply see (by looking, NOT feeling or thinking) that feeling that or anything else, like pain or pleasure, is simply Consciousness, the "Energy-Intelligence" of the Absolute Non-Dual, is simply a bubbling up appearing in the always already Awareness-Presence

That is arising AS Consciousness, and all content— and NOT separate from Consciousness in any way except that "thinking" (another bubbling up of Energy-Intelligence patterning into a thought-form) makes it into "two."

Me and my shadow.

So: WHO is "feeling this?" And WHO is asking the question!?

Find out. Trace that "I" thought all the way back to its Silent Source. Then it is annihilated in the heatless smokeless fire of Self-Knowing Awareness.

Although that realization is in no way complete as the pain in my side indicated very sharply.

THERE IS NO REALIZATION.

Seeing the actuality of that IS itself 'Realization.'

Who would realize? Inquire within! Understanding This... that there is NO such "event" as enlightenment for anyone, is the beginning of the non-dual wisdom... as Nisargadatta pointed out and Bob verified, that Understanding which begins in "mind" actually burns away the idea of a "mind."

That Understanding is the beginning of the end of it all — in the appearance of a process, the phantom "thinker," the "mind," evaporates, so to say. It's just seen to never have had any actual existence in Reality. It was all a thought-story... the "Tale told by an idiot."

Then (NOW) The gateless gate opens and no one enters nowhere. Now Here. Looking back, there IS no gate! All there is, IS, Here and Now. That is all.

It looks like this book is generating a LOT of good energy and people are benefiting, including "me."

I found that by sticking with it despite the pain and the intense psychological suffering that made me want to commit suicide, and staying in contact with the I Am appearing as Bob, John, my doctor, and the others in Bob's 'network' that the identity was totally and irrevocably seen through

Now nothing is wrong here any more. (It never was in Reality.) It, as you already understand, is not an event, or a realization, or enlightenment. All that is a story told by a seeker still trying to avoid his or her own essential emptiness... the No Thing.

Once it is seen that you actually ARE what is sought, the seeker dies and the game is over. Then there is just the spontaneous celebration of livingness, aliveness, uncaused Being-Awareness-Peace, as It is. I Love you as the I Am that I Am and "you" are.

Stay in touch until there is no one left to do or not do THAT, Okay? Then the Absolute, Non-Conceptual I Am will effortlessly and spontaneously share through that pattern of Energy-Intelligence called (only in thought!) a body-mind with the label "Gary." "Charlie" and "Gary" are thought forms only, just appearing in the One... Presence Awareness... the pure non-dual I Am-Ness. Stay with THAT. Abiding AS That, there is Peace.

Much Love, and thanks for writing!

37. The Self Is Already Realized

Q: Any insights as to any practice to self-realization? I do a lot of research and reading, such as Wei Wu Wei and Nisargadatta. Thank you.

The Self is already realized. You exist and are aware, right? That simple Presence Awareness is the Self... the non-dual one-without-a-second, simple awareness itself. So from this we can see that any practices to "get self-realization" are occurring in that already always presence that we ARE... and could tend to reinforce the sense of a separate entity that needs to get somewhere other then right here.

There is an awareness that there is seemingly a sense of a "person" who seeks self-realization, yes? This sense needs to be investigated. Is there really a separate entity in the organism? Or is there simply an unexamined thought-feeling that "I am a person in a world?"

Look deeply into this belief in a "me" and you will find that apart from a thought arising presently in Awareness - that which you ARE - the "me" has no substance or reality. And what is a thought? Just a movement of energy, forming, like a cloud, in the space of Awareness, and dissolving. Like a dream.

Look into these things, understanding that you already are what you seek. Don't try to figure things out... the answer is NOT in the mind! Awareness, Presence, is shining here and now, BEFORE the mind arises. Without Awareness not a thing can exist. Just see that THAT is your true nature.

38. Try To NOT Be

I am trying to get to the bottom of this even after knowing (who knows?) that I don't exist as an entity and only "I am" exists (Awareness). Who knows? That is what I am trying to get to.

You are already pointing it out to yourself, in asking, "Who is this I?" And "Who knows?" And realizing the phantom nature of the "I-Entity." Keep that alive.

Often, as reports go, just seeing the false as false is sufficient for Oneness to work within the so-called "you" cooking that "I" from the inside out, like a microwave oven. You have seen that there is no actual entity, even though the mind thought story arising in Presence) SAYS there is; right?

Now what?

The bottom line? Nothing. Nothing is "next." THIS, AS IT IS RIGHT HERE AND RIGHT NOW, FOR "YOU" AS YOU ARE, IS IT, Russell! ONENESS is appearing as a "me" and all its foibles, doubts, stories, confusions... ALL of that is Oneness. Not Two.

There is no more that can be done (because there is no one to "do" or "not do" anything.) For starters just see if that can be accepted by the mind, at first. As Maharaj said, "Use your mind to know your mind. It is perfectly legitimate and also the best preparation for going beyond the mind."

Refuse to budge from that space. Then Presence Awareness, which is never actually missing, is seen to be always shining. Dig deeper and THAT will be seen to be never missing. In any event, I ask you again, can you deny your own Being? Try to NOT BE. Impossible! Totally impossible! So quit buying into the bullshit your head is telling you. Just cut it out. By steadfastly refusing to believe in it any more. Stay with the Real... I Am. Add NOTHING TO That! Catch the mind in the act and bring forth the full stop at I Am.

Even though, after claiming that my search is over and my true nature (Oneness) has revealed itself, the phantom entity still lives on.

There is always a problem with a claim, an assertion, the search is over... so long as it is over for a someone making that assertion. But look: many, including "me," have been through that phase. See it for what it is... the ego asserting itself to "keep its job" of making you a small, limited thing called "me." When the search ends, this "I" is seen to have never been real in any way shape or form!

When "that" happens, it is simply that nothing happened, to no one. The seeker, the search and the process all dissolve so to speak... leaving, just This. Exactly as it is.

Now: Does an entity actually live on? Really? Is that TRUE? Who is MAKING it true? You are, in ignoring the always evident fact of your own Being-Presence.

On the one hand, I know full well that I (Russell), the entity, does not exist but on the other hand, the I (entity) is still alive and appearing as real.

That "entity" is NOT alive. The mind is simply telling you that it is alive. And it is merely a belief... the acceptance of a thing without rigorous investigation and the finding that there is no EVIDENCE for any actual existence of this so called thing called "Russell."

Apart from the alive-NESS, Presence Awareness, how can it even APPEAR? So yes, there is the appearance... but the incomplete investigation into the actual truth or falsity of that entity is still causing some confusion and doubts... for itself only! Is Awareness, your simple Being-ness, ever affected by those thought stories? You are simply taking the false to be real. Don't refuse to look more deeply than you ever have! See the dream as a dream. What never changes? Being-Awareness. You are that. Period.

I know that this false self will continue to exist due to conditioning and habit and will die when the physical body does but I am struggling with this 'two-ness.' The thought "I am this" keeps appearing on its own and occasionally the "I am" (true nature) is revealed but the false self shows its face soon after.

WHO knows this? That is also nothing more than an appearance of a story believed in... but in actuality it is nothing but thought-clouds assembling and dissipating on the blank screen of Pure Awareness – Being. What are "you" excluding from Oneness? Can you see how silly that is? It is One... Not Two... Non- Duality. That leaves nothing out. NOTHING.

I know that you will respond by saying investigate who this I is, get to the root of it, see if it stands on its own, etc.... but I still find this entity when I use the mind to see that there is no mind. I know that I can't grasp this with the mind, that it is outside the mind, but the mind is the only tool I have to do the investigation.

Totally false. How do you know what response will arise!? Do you even know what your next thought will be?

The "correct" tool is the awareness itself. NOT the "mind"... there is no such thing as mind. That is just another word. A four-letter word!

As another friend wrote me recently:

Yeah, I get it. Ask "Who am I?" then actually look and see. Looking and seeing is really very easy. After dismissing the world, the body, and thought as who I am, there isn't anything left. :-)

I answered:

And there never WAS any "entity"... No Thing is left, and then even THAT goes! :-))

Man, this is really messing up my mind.
Charlie, I am stuck. I don't exist..

You DO exist! Just not a separate "thing" called "I." THAT is the key point being overlooked. You ARE. Being is undeniable and unavoidable. You cannot NOT be! Haven't you noticed?!? So the story "I Am stuck" is being bought. Use the sword of clear looking (NOT in the mind, figuring it out will NEVER work) to see the DISTINCTION between "I AM" and "Stuck." You ARE. STOP THERE and STAY PUT.

And yet I sense that I, the entity, does exist.

And that is the bullshit "you" as a so called thinker are buying into. You are conning yourself, dear friend. Stop it. Awareness IS, the "entity" is NOT. You have it exactly backward, as the mind is trained to believe since the false core "I" thought arrived and was believed when you were two or three.

Yes, this is all coming out of my mind, which supposedly does not exist. What the fuck is going on? Sorry, but this is how I feel at the moment. It looks like the belief in this false self is very strong but how do I see for what it is?

By LOOKING rather than trying to figure out how. Now LOOK! WHO needs to know HOW? Just the natural effortless looking without belief or concept... in the same way that seeing happens naturally of all the appearance before the eyes, independent of any thought that "I see..."

As I am writing this, I see that the mind is doing all this and I (as awareness) find it amusing...

You as awareness are NOT either a subject who is amused or an object that can be known by the mind. All false beliefs! There is simply nothing real about any of that. You are simply addicted to being a story. You are the star of your own sad, sad story. Get real with the looking and cut through this crap. Give it up. All this "figuring it out" will never bring you to the Peace that you are in Reality.

Awareness simply IS... and THAT is No Thing that can be grasped. IT does or knows or sees nothing. It is Consciousness appearing as a knower that is amused. NOT Awareness its Self. That is an Empty, Blank Screen, to make an analogy. But don't get stuck on any of these concepts. They are useless as mind fodder. Use until they bring fruition and then discard!

It soon fades away and I am back to suffering.

Again totally false. How can your own knowingness that you exist, you ARE, ever fade? Your belief in the story "It fades" is the only issue to be dealt with... and that belief is pinned to the "thinking" that you are a thing, a body-mind, an "I". All the I is, is a thought!

Who does not see this? You argue incessantly for your unreal cage of limitations which are nothing but thoughts. Such a story! STOP! Stop Telling That Story!

How can I see this false self as false, Charlie, How??? The answer is you can't because the I (entity) is not real but try telling that to someone who thinks he is real. I can't seem to surrender to Oneness, my true nature. I must love the story of me too much.

Exactly. It is an addiction of mind to itself. It can only be cut asunder by the ruthless investigation into the actuality of that till it is seen beyond a shred of doubt that it (the "me") never WAS real. But the mind is the machinery looping back on itself in endless questions. WHO is asking the questions? Find out!

But there is too much suffering there. I do want to come home to my true nature but it appears that the I (entity), the false self, does not want to give up yet, I guess.

Who wants!?
When the suffering got so intense here that there came a commitment to really getting to the source of that suffering, the seeing began to open, and in the simple Awareness the Consciousness dawned, "Oh, yeah, I AM That, and have never NOT been That. Cognizing emptiness. Nothing but That."

As I reviewed this letter before clicking the send button, I noticed that I sure used lots of "I"s in this email. So I guess my question is how to get out of this I that I believe I am.

Who needs to get out of that which has no existence? You are in the mind game, the conceptual loop. Seeing that, can you really buy into the belief in that?

You are like a sailor (no pun intended) believing you cannot sail out too far, or your boat, and you, will fall off the edge of the absolutely FLAT EARTH (as it was believed for eons).

What's left? Perhaps you might simply give up the search. You have failed. There is nothing more to do. Or not do. Have a beer and watch TV, and forget all this non-duality stuff.

There is NO HOPE, dear friend. NONE. It is your belief in someday and a me that will get something it does not have and needs, that keeps you in chains. Embrace the despair and resignation, and when the spirit moves you, INQUIRE.

Who are you?

39. Who Is This "I" That You Claim to Be?

<u>Follow-up</u>... Russell writes, *Okay, I've had enough, I think I am finally ready to inquire and investigate as to who is this "I" that I claim to be. I am doing this exercise as I am writing this email to you. The question is: Do I exist as a separate entity? Does Charlie exist as a separate entity? Do others exist as separate entities? Well, the answer is No.*

Not bad! Now, see that any "answer" is more tomfoolery! The answer arises in the mind. ASK, "To whom did that word 'no' arise?" And a natural follow-up to that could be, "Who wants to understand and get what?" And... "Who is asking whom?" And "Who is watching the play of the mind?" And "Who is watching the watcher?" Keep real there (here) that in apparent "time" Asking happens, then LOOKING. Asking in the mind comes first. Then just look into the presence and see what arises. Reject all answers: not that, not that!

In what does all that appear as the play of Consciousness? That Absolute Pure Non-Conceptual Presence Awareness. That is the Silent Knower named by the apparent thought process as "I Am."

We are Oneness (one without the second) living in the world of duality.

Not quite. "Oneness" itself is another conceptual illusion appearing real. And there is no we and no world and no duality in the Real. WE are not "living." Livingness simply IS. Appearing as all that seems to BE. In actuality "we" are the No Thing from and in which all that is, arises, a throb of aliveness, life itself. It IS. It cannot be expressed. Language is dualism. The One does not "know"... just see that the Not Knowing is a pointer to the actual... Presence Awareness.

All words are ultimately crap... but they do serve as pointers from The Absolute to its Self, appearing as both a dreamer and all the dreamed characters and their universes.

Here is a pointer from Ramana Maharshi: "The thought 'who am I?' will destroy all other thoughts, and like the stick used for stirring the burning pyre, it will itself in the end get destroyed. Then, there will arise Self-realization."

Try this on: The Absolute cannot know itself. It IS that "Cognizing Emptiness" that, as Consciousness, SEES all that is, and as the Absolute, is the Silent Stillness before the joyous expansion of its Self into Self and Other-Than-Self.

We are all just clouds in the sky but our true nature is the sun, always shining, Presence Awareness.

You just keep on persisting in trying to tell the "right story!" There is no right answer. ALL answers are crap.

In Pure Awareness, there IS No we, no our, no clouds, no sky, no true nature, no sun. That is all appearance... objects, words, concepts. Real Absolute True-Nature is inexpressible and unimaginable. And, YES. NON-Conceptual Pure Awareness IS Self-Shining. YES. That Thou Art.

Now, what just popped up in my head is, okay, but I still feel like a separate entity even though I know this. So I guess my next step will have to be who claims this ? It appears to be the thought "I". Just a thought that claims ownership of its existence as real.

Whose head? Where is that? It is only a thought!

Feelings are also concepts, appearances. Pure Non-Conceptual Presence Awareness cognizes all, including "feelings." You, the pure Awareness, perceive a feeling as Consciousness, and then (it seems) take it on board as MY feeling. The personalizing is the issue; dissolve that with inquiry. WHO "knows this!?" All "okay, yes, buts" are more story arising presently in this that you are... Awareness its Self.

The next thought that is now arising is, how do thoughts appear? Who is pulling the strings? There is no answer to this question. So, is this all coming from nothingness? Something coming from Nothing. How can this be? So now I ask , what is "something?" Is it real or is it just an illusion, a dream, taken as

real? Scientists do agree that our body, physicality, is really just vibrating ener-
gy —Not Solid.

All good insight. And not any more real that any other thought... but fair pointers! Let the insight reveal the questioner, the knower, the Self. And notice that ALL "how" questions reveal the still-believed-in "person" who "wants to know how." WHO is it that wants or needs to know how anything happens? All happens. Chit (Consciousness) Happens! All how and why stories are prompts to the mind to keep telling itself its own story. If you want to know how or why, find a religion. If you want freedom and an end to questions, the questioner, and all suffering and doubts, and all else, ask WHO.

Hmm... okay then, who I am is nothing appearing as something. Boy! I guess I had it backwards all my life. What I claimed to be real is really unreal.

Stop trying to figure this out! Just see right now that that "I" which "had it backwards" and "my life" is another fiction arising presently. Nobody had anything backwards in actual fact... there is nobody to get it wrong. That is all more "enlightened story" told by a seeker trying to end his own seeking in the mind.

Get that "I" out of the mix. Who IS that? The answer is not in the mind. The answer is non-conceptual Silence. The eternal still point of the turning wheel of livingness. The hub of the wheel... emptiness. That emptiness supports the wheel but That is Not the wheel. I, the Absolute, alone, IS, and all sprouts from that. And those are Not Two.

So, I will now try to get to the root of when did this mistaken identity first occur? I guess around the age of two. This is when just seeing, just hearing, became "I see", "I hear."

It doesn't matter when. Who will try? Just do the questions! Who Am I?

Only see that this identity is false. As Nisargadatta said, "See the false AS false. That is all that is needed." When is TIME? What is time? Time is mind. Thought. The concept "time" appears in awareness and is made real only by the investment of BELIEF that the thought is real. NO thought is real. Quit "trying" and just LOOK.

Russell, the entity, was born.

Absolutely False. The "entity" was NEVER born. A body-mind formed from a single sperm cell and an ovum and naturally was grown by intelligence-energy into a fetus, then a formed object called "a baby" came out of another object called "mother." Then a name – only a thought! – arose in Pure Awareness and was attached to the organism.

Now that organism has a label and is seen by parents as a real separate person. By parents who also believed they are real separate persons. A couple-three years later the new thought "I am" appeared... the story that "I am me, that is Mother, all that 'out there' is my world, this is my body, my thoughts – TIME IS" was born... and taken to be real. That is all. And all THIS is also a story!

I became a living separate entity. And what followed was years and years of conditioning to make this belief as solid as possible. Hurray for the Ego!!! The ego is alive and doing well until nonduality came into the picture. The ego is now fighting for its life and will do whatever is necessary to keep itself alive.

Just see that that whole dissertation is nothing more than a story, appearing and believed. The appearance is no problem. The believing IS the problem. Root out that belief in a believer! Who or what IS that?

I recall, you once said: The mind is a liar and will do anything to keep itself alive. How true. I am now beginning to see this. When I see some clarity, it always tries to slip through the back door and usually succeeds to keep its identity alive and suffering is usually present.

That was a pointer ONLY, to a particular appearance, a patterning as a stubborn phantom-seeker, and NOT "True." There

IS no "mind." Just thoughts arising presently. All this is just more story. Is any of that TRUE? Find the storyteller. Where is it? Who is that? WHO?

Well, I guess the game is now over. The mind (ego) is exposed for what it is. The great cosmic joke. Indeed, it was a great roller coaster ride!! And that is that. The end.

Every story begins with "Once upon a time," doesn't it? And when time is seen as a false concept appearing real, then the end and the beginning disappear into the Absolute Perfect Silence of your True Nature. No Thing appearing as Every Thing.

Thank you Charlie, you have been a great help for telling it as it is. No bullshit.

40. Praise and Blame!

After sending us the glowing praise, *"Thank you Charlie, you have been a great help for telling it as it is. No bullshit,"* our buddy Russell comes up with: *"This is what is bubbling up at the moment."*

Sounds good, like he really IS done with his seeking! But soon it all is seen as the ignorance of wannabe trying to look wise.

If I can be honest with you, which I have been doing all along in my emails to you, I must ask you a few questions. Your response to the last few emails surprised me

Oh? Who is surprised? Do you know that?

Russell me lad, What you call "honesty" is your endless *story.* There is no such thing as "honesty or dishonesty" apart from the stories you persist in telling me and Annette.

When this latest epistle from you arrived I found I had some extra time, and– out of some sort of masochistic compassion I guess –it came up to write a response.

Don't count on that happening again, though. Until you show some respect, and a willingness to *listen,* and see what can be seen from these pointings.

It appears that you took [a letter written to me on a bulletin board] as a personal attack.

You have written before about that. I declined to respond. Now here you are again, still beating THAT dead horse? Jeez. So what if, at that "time, David's letter was perceived as an 'attack'?"

At that "time" (a dream) there was still a not-yet-seen-to-be-false "me" in play. That "me" was quite thin-skinned. No more, bubba. Bring on any "attack" you like.

Nothing can touch That Which Is Real. It is an Impersonal Awareness, NO person exists and never did. Here, there, anywhere, or any-when.

Now as to why I did not choose to print the thing? First off, what in you is there to care? Secondly as I did tell you, it was old obsolete dead news. All story. WHO is telling you that your stories mean any thing? Those, like you, are Empty and Meaningless. Full Stop. Until That becomes your 24/7 direct knowing, you'll keep on and on with the stories, hoping to... what? Get some attention?

Your response to that email indicated that [a me taking offense]. You claim that the search is over. I believed you so I sent that email thinking you were beyond that

The search, the suffering, IS over, since early July 2006. (Actually only Just Now.) Before that, there was, in the dream-appearance, a "me" CLAIMING the search to be over, not realizing that in fact it was not, at that "time." So what? That is what IS. Anyway it's all just a stupid story arising right here and right now.

LOOK! Who Cares? Are you suffering? If not, why are you writing this to me? If so, who is suffering? Strap that Quest on for real, bro.

There is no need to prove to any so-called "other" that suffering has ended. I really do NOT care whether "I" am "believed" or not. That's all agreement-approval crap. I could care less whether you or anyone approves or agrees with the expression that flows out of this bag of piss and shit called Charlie. Who doesn't SEE THAT? Nothing can touch or affect That Which IS... True-Essence. Period.

When you do not care either (so to say) there will be unimaginable freedom, but not for you. And that day is Here Now. ONLY here now.

I first took your response as Oneness speaking, pointing that I am attached to my ego self, but my gut feeling tells me that it was Charlie (ego self) responding and attacking Russell (another ego self).

Who has the feeling? See that persistent belief in someone – someone else. It's a projection, guy. Pointing fingers, judging stories, and making endless accusations, no matter how many times they are signed "with love," or another sucking up statement, are crap. Until there is TRULY no Russell, have a look at what is motivating you to write this stuff to me, Annette and any others you are pestering.

My investigation and inquiring to "Who am I?", the only question worth asking, is still going on. It is clear that all is appearing on the face of "No Thing."

Quite right. As I have tried my best to point out to you. So why do you go off on these rants?

It is also clear that the ego self will continue to live on until the physical body dies.

This is totally false. THERE IS NO SUCH THING as an "ego-self"!!

With one exception, and this is a crucial pointer,

Who says so? Crucial to whom? Why are you still playing guru-sage?

It is not believed to be real and seen through with investigation.

O, Your Supreme Holiness! Thou art so learned and wise. You know everything!
All your knowing is crap!
WHO is doing this writing? Who is typing this here and reading this here? Who is the crucial pointer for?
You are turning friends away. Why not stop with all the argumentativeness?

The ego self does not disappear instantly.

Totally False. The ego-self is NONEXISTENT. It is only a THOUGHT. Unreal and powerless. That inauthentic "you" is powerless to *not* write this stuff. WHO ARE YOU? Shut up and bake!
Who Am I? What Am I Really?

NO Answer. That ends all the arguing and being right that you are so attached to as you will drop into the abyss. Then you may truly be able to reach out to others still suffering.

You are still hiding in your stories. This is a shame. It is so needless...

Here is a poem from Hafiz, in case you take umbrage (as the ego might very well do so.)

Love wants to reach out and
            break all your teacup talk of God.

If you had the courage and could give
The Beloved His choice,
some nights He would just
drag you around the room by your hair,

ripping from your grip all those
toys [stories] in the world,
That bring you no joy.

Love sometimes gets tired of speaking sweetly,
And wants to rip to shreds
All your erroneous notions of truth.

This makes you fight within yourself,
dear one, <u>and with others</u>

Causing the world to weep on too many fine days.

God wants to manhandle us,
lock us inside a tiny room with Himself,
and practice his dropkick.

The Beloved sometimes wants to do us
A great favor:
Hold us upside down
and shake all the nonsense out.

But when we hear He is in
such a "playful drunken mood,"

Most everyone I know
quickly packs their bags,
and hightails it out of town.

So, my freind, read and argue... or get the pointless point...
who cares?

*Anyway, you can respond back by chewing out my head, or by compas-
sion, or not respond at all. Whatever you do, I accept with love. Thank you. I am
still a fan of your web site. Well done!!*

Compassion is not loving kindness or pity. Compassion
does **not** buy your story. Compassion is a Divine Fire that burns
out the bullshit that keeps you suffering. TRUE compassion is utterly RUTHLESS. Shiva! The destroyer of ignorance.

As to the rest, ho hum. All just more of your endless sucking
up. Stop it! It is NOT attractive, and it shows you as the fake you
are. I do have a kind of empathy for that, having "once upon a time"
been where you are.

Certain Authentic ones, like Bob Adamson and John
Wheeler, offer a compassion that is truly RUTHLESS. That brooks
no stories and will not tolerate a loser who will not see.

Thank What Is!

If you can take it, then take it. If not who cares?

Follow-up

Thank you, that hit home.

Back to praise! Hey Russell, just stop writing and telling
your stories here and there, and go BAKE. Keep asking yourself
"Who Am I?" until you DROP.

41. Listen As I Am, Hearing I Am — Heart To Heart.

Mark wrote, I just started reading your book, and my initial response is: "Wow!" Since you updated it, I have a good excuse to begin again at the beginning.

Happy to hear the book is working for you. I look forward to hearing more feedback as you work with the pointers. (Or as they work on "you!" :-))

Tuesday I'll be flying to England for a four-day retreat. I'm probably guilty of trying to storm heaven's gates, but it feels like the right thing to be doing right now. I want to be done. I know you've been helped by Tony. Any thoughts/advice in terms of my time with him?

Have FUN. And ask, who needs a retreat? ASK, "Who are these teachers" and "Who Am I?"

All there is, is the I Am that YOU are in truth. Don't listen as a "person hearing another person"... that will bear no fruit. (NOT that there IS actually any "fruit" to "come forth!") And, as a tip from no one to no one, focus on the Energy-Intelligence *from* where the words and feelings pour into the space of Consciousness from the pure Oneness – IMPERSONAL Being-Awareness – rather than comparing concepts and trying to sort it all out in the (dualistic thinking) mind.

Hey, have a good look! Who is this "I" that is "trying to storm anything"? Heaven is nonexistent! You as an "entity" are nonexistent. Full stop.

REALLY, just see that right here right now, "it" is already "done." And all ideas or feelings that mount a thought-argument against that ARE the ego-mind trying to survive. It can only survive in the absence of looking for it... whereupon it is found to be the phantom of the opera called "my life." Ultimately there ain't no "I" to "get done." AND, there is no way to escape your own Beingness, is there? Try to NOT BE! Impossible. Is that not seen? Who says?

Mark, you have already seen that the I Am of NON-conceptual Presence Awareness is undeniable and unavoidable... stay with

That, and as long as there appears to be a looker, look deeply into and *from* That "backwards" for a separate observer or witness... then it is found out... there is no such animal. And Oneness reveals its Self as nothing and Everything, right here and right now as Timeless Being... NOT TWO. One-Without-A-Second. That, Thou ART.

Of course until that is SEEN (and it is also seen that there never was a seeker and nothing happened to no one) then my pointer is, LOOK into the Space-like Awareness and see if there is a real, substantial seeker. There is a paradox in that, of course. As a Zen Master noted, Paradox and Confusion are the guardians at the Gateless Gate. Embrace ALL that is including paradox, confusion, and apparently contradictory messages and all will be as it already is... perfect!

42. Are You Happy, Charlie?

Alan asks, "are you happy, Charlie?"

The relative (duality) answer is, "Yes, I am. Blessedly, there is no more suffering."

The Appearing (Consciousness) answer is... "There IS Happiness." Uncaused joy.

The Absolute (non-duality) answer is...

Silence – Stillness. Just That.

Okay?

But who cares?

Are YOU happy? If not let's chat.

43. It's Hard To Accept That Suffering Can End

Q: What a delight to see that you've rediscovered "the home you never left!" If I may, though, I'd like to ask a very blunt question about suffering. You, Sailor Bob, and others talk about how suffering ends once identity as Presence Awareness, rather than a separate mind/body entity, is recognized. But somehow that's hard to accept. If my daughter becomes ill, if my wife runs off with the mailman, if I get fired from my job, if the bills are due and I can't pay them, there's going to be suffering.

A: The question is, for whom? If there is no identification with "the person" then where can anything that arises be fixated on? Only an entity with language can think "something's wrong"... which is the essence of suffering. When the entity is seen to be false the whole paradigm collapses and *all there is, is what is.* Of course what is can include pain. But suffering is another matter.

As far as accepting the concept, one word of advice: DON'T. All concepts can be debated endlessly; the nature of language is dual. Look for yourself, use the words as pointers... rather than trying to agree or disagree, look at the pointer as though you *really* don't know. Because, you don't! All knowledge is ignorance. Our own beliefs (and in my case, my arrogance) trip us up more often than you know. And keep the understanding before you that the answer is not in the mind.

Now, let's distinguish pain from suffering: If the daughter becomes ill, or the wife leaves, there may be emotional pain as part of that story. But not suffering, which is a secondary mechanistic involvement by a "me" that thinks "This Should Not Be."

Finally, let's take another look at what a "me" is. That me is a thought-story, with emotion and "filled with sound and fury." But "signifying nothing." In the manifestation, there ARE appearing separate bodies. That appearance does not necessarily change. What is gone, in this Understanding, is the ENTITY. Bodies hurt. Nisargadatta groaned in pain. But when asked, "Are you in great pain?" His response makes the distinction clear: "There IS great pain." In other words, the pain is not taken on board by the entity, because the entity no longer exists with any fixation.

The thought I is not the "True I." Look into the fact of your very own beingness – Presence Awareness – and tell me if there is actually any person in that, apart from an idea, a movement of energy?

Are you saying that, from where you sit, such events would be no more significant than whether the milk in your refrigerator spoils or not?

There might be crying over spoiled milk or the rotten wife or sick child, but not with any fixation or ideation that "what is should not be..." The events would be happenings... for no one. Like watching a movie.

Let me put it another way: it would make no difference to "you" whether you're sleeping on a park bench or on a soft bed under a down comforter? From "my" perspective, if this body-mind organism were on the park bench, I don't doubt there would be suffering!

But right now you are not on a park bench, and if you tell the truth, you do not actually KNOW what would be experienced, whether there would be pain or not, whether there would still seem to be a "me" in the story that said this sucks. There certainly can be preferences as part of the organism's functioning. But, and this is the bottom line, IF THERE IS NO PERSON, THERE CAN BE NO SUFFERING. What's wrong with right now unless you think about it?

Thanks for your web site, and no sarcasm is intended by these questions. I really want to know!

No disrespect or sarcasm on this end either, but REALLY... Who is asking the question? Rather than speculating endlessly and throwing all sorts of what ifs up and grinding away with the mind, understand that the answer is NOT in the mind. Then root out the source and cause of all suffering... the belief in "me." Look for that one that can suffer, find that one... if you can. All that troubles us is our own imagination. See that, and all questions evaporate... along with the questioner.

Thanks for a fine question.

<u>Follow-up</u>

Thanks for a beautiful, clear — and very quick — answer! Yes, I can see how I'm engaging in a lot of mental grinding. And how the suffering comes DI-RECTLY from the thought, "This should not be."

Good!

And how -- in my case -- there's an extra dose of suffering from endless thinking along the lines of, "If only I had paid more attention to my wife, she wouldn't be with the mailman now! What a fool I was!" But if there's no "me," then there was no one to pay more attention, do a better job, take more care, etc. It all just happened, right?

It all APPEARED to happen. But look, right now, and see... who is thinking? Find the thinker. You cannot! It's a phantom, an imaginary "friend," nothing more substantial than a mental construct. And where is there any past... or any "me"... unless there is thought, imagination... a story of "me" and "my life?" Then there is a good laugh: What wife? What mailman? It was all a story, a figment of imagination.

Right now, this moment, where is any of that real, other than as a movement of the energy of Awareness-Presence forming into letters-words-concepts and a fictional reference point called "me"? Then the seeing happens... aha! NOTHING happened. And right now this too is nothing, happening to no one. THAT can NEVER be grasped by the mind, the storyteller.

And as you said, I can just watch the movie — laughing or crying, as the case may be — but knowing it's just a movie that I can't jump into (because there's no "I") and somehow affect the outcome.

So far so good. Now I also sense you are already taking this to the next level of insight: WHO watches the movie? WHO is "do-ing a lot of mental grinding?" Who is the owner of "my" life story, who is the owner of "my" body, "my" world? Through investigation into the reality (or NOT) of this "me" get the "Me-and-mine" out of the picture and what is left is Being, No Thing. Freedom. Then there is no "me" left to tell that story... poof.

It's really starting to make sense . . . .

Ultimately it will make no sense because the seeing is clear that there is no mind to make sense of it... I suspect you are essentially clear, and then the attempt to put it into words falls short as it must because the word is never what the word points to. We can't drink the word water, and the word I is not the actual I – Consciousness, Being.

It's great to hear from you how the Understanding is taking hold! Keep in touch if you want to; I would love to hear more from you as this natural freedom unfolds. If questions or doubts arise get them out on the table and get them resolved. As a famous guru once said, the job of the mind is to think and doubt. But see the mind as false and it can never trouble you again!

Non-conceptual, ever fresh, self-shining, self-knowing Presence Awareness... just this and nothing else. That, thou art.

44: The Endless Myths Of Enlightenment

A visitor here asked, "Isn't it as [a famous so-called 'Advaita Teacher'] stated, that 'For the sage, these things no longer happen: Anger, Hatred, Guilt and Fear?'"

That's yet another "enlightenment Myth." First off, there is no "Sage"... that is a concept born of a dualistic mind that still thinks in terms of two... "sage" and "non-sage" (or "Jnani and Aj-nani" in Hindu parlance.)

To be blunt, it's crap.

I have been trapped in those kinds of concepts until recently. Now, when anger happens it happens. It comes and goes, like a thunderstorm. But have you noticed that a thunderstorm doesn't hang around after its fury is spent and gripe to itself that "I should-n't have stormed about like that! It scares animals and little kids. I feel so bad about it!" THAT is called guilt. And guilt is added by a judging mind that says in essence, what IS "should not be" and what happened "Should have been different."

The mind has all sorts of expectations and ideals and pictures of what a "Liberated One" is like. How he or she acts, dresses, moves, what kind of music he or she likes ("new-age" soft songs or "bhajans" or other fake holy nonsense.) And the emotions are never supposed to arise. I have nothing against any of that. But I do NOT take it as a "sign" of any "sagehood!" That is just bullshit.

Anger can arise... the difference is, when there is no "fixat-ing self-center," no "me", to take delivery of it, it comes and goes without the overlay of a commenting "personal self" that makes it out to be wrong, and feels a whole new suffering emotional state of guilt.

Now: Guilt, in fact, cannot come up unless there is a sense of "I did that and I shouldn't have!" So guilt is gone from the pic-ture. Hatred also cannot arise. There may be anger and there may be an expression of it, but that again that comes and goes without a sense of an "authoring entity" or a "personal doer." However, regret certainly can arise. The difference is, when there is regret there is no sense that "it should not be." Then what may also arise is an apology for something that happened, also as a spontaneous arising, uncaused by any entity.

So far as fear is concerned, for me there is no longer any fear of an imagined future, no matter how grim. I have had a recurring fear of losing all my money and ending up old, homeless, broke, rained on, and sick as a junkyard dog without a junkyard for shelter and an owner to feed it. That fear is gone, even though the thought-story sometimes arises out of habitual, conditioned mind stuff. But when it is not taken delivery of, then there is simply no fear about it, as it is seen clearly to be nothing substantial or real, just the dreamed character having dream appearance right here in Presence Awareness. As "Sailor" Bob continually points out, "What's Wrong with Right Now... unless you think about it?"

That saying really resonates for me: Notice the use of the word "you." When there is no you, thoughts are naturally seen as Awareness-Presence arising as consciousness and forming the thought of a me for whom there is something wrong. That is the core belief that happened when the seeming "separation" occurred in the small child.

The "me" is essentially unreal, and once seen as such, that belief-story is unable to attach to any entity itself and so it simply passes, as it burns away in the heatless smokeless fire of the Absolute, Presence Awareness, like a cloud burnt away by that ever-present heat of the sun.

By the same token, fear as a totally natural response of the organism to a threat, such as a car heading toward you on a collision course at high speed, can arise, and at the same time there will be spontaneous action taken (by no one) to avoid the disintegration of that organism.

I have experienced this: I was driving at 70 MPH on a freeway one day, and was distracted by a roadside event on the other side. By the time my attention reverted to where the car I was in was headed, it was seen that I was only about fifty feet away from a car in my lane that had slowed to about 20 MPH! The wheel was turned and brakes applied and corrections to steering made and the nearly inevitable collision averted... by no one. Immediately, within seconds, there was a heart pounding sense of fear. That fear was caused by a story told after the fact of the averted accident...

and I saw (it was seen) that the fear was simply a stored response to the threat – stored as a memory. So all the fear which arose in this case was memory. An after-the-fact response to a now only imagined threat to survival (to me, memory and imagination are really cut from the same cloth...mind-stuff only.)

Another time, just a couple of weeks ago, I was half asleep when I heard a loud BANG. Above and behind me. (I still don't know what that was.) I jumped about a foot and my heart raced, and I noticed the mind labeled that experience fear. It was over in an instant and this time there was no aftermath. It came and was gone like the cloud.

The point is, there is simply NO "litmus test" for whether or not the non-event of the dissolution of the false entity has happened through a particular organism. Don't buy any of the myths; they lead us to look for the keys where they aren't.

45. If There IS No One How Do You Investigate?

Paul asks, "How do you investigate, when there is an I that is investigating? I mean if there is nothing to look for then how do you investigate and what am I investigating if there is no I or me?"

That's the paradox. There is no me — yet as long as "you" believe there is a you, who asks "how do you investigate, that entity has got to be put to the test of self-investigation.

Another correspondent beautifully articulated the short version: "Yeah, I get it. Ask 'Who am I?' then actually look and see. Looking and seeing is really very easy. After dismissing the world, the body, and thought as who I am, there isn't anything left."

It's a paradox. There is no you, AND what is needed is the looking "by you." Paradox and confusion are pointed to as the guardians at the gateless gate of seeing who you really are! Some dismiss the paradox as a contradiction. It IS a contradiction, a dilemma... to the mind. And a paradox is never resolved! There are two opposing concepts and that can never be resolved... mind says one is right and the other is wrong. That is duality... at its most (apparently) destructive. A paradox is DISSOLVED (not resolved) in the Light of Not Knowing (there's another paradox!) Chew on this. See what is seen.

Just really stop now and SEE that looking is NOT a mental exercise. That is the mind's way of co-opting the inquiry and putting itself in an endless loop. "Who Am I?" "I Am." "Who Am I?" "I Am." "Who Am I?" "I Am." "Who Am I?" "I Am." All that produces is headaches and frustration. The LOOKING is natural effortless seeing, as seeing happens through the eyes but the idea "I see" comes after, as an "overlay" on the plain ordinary Awareness that cognizes all that appears in the space.

The main issue for me is this solid identity that I have with a me and the second part is that my mind is so busy, so analytical, that I can't seem to get out of my mind, does that make sense? What to do? The mind is the cause of my suffering.

As long as there remains a belief that there is a "doer" who can "do something," put that do-er to work asking WHO? Who is the "me?" Who is thinking "I am a solid identity?" And "I can't get out of 'my mind'?" On investigation it is finally (in apparent time) seen through as no more substantial that a holographic image. Shut off the laser light and where is the hologram!? It never was. That is analogous to the so-called mind, which is just a bunch of thoughts, all tied onto and sprouting from a root concept called "I."

The "I" thought is the ONLY culprit. Trace back back back by effortless looking and you will see (it will be seen by no one) that it never had any independent existence apart from the light of Awareness. And when you, so to say, turn 180 degrees and look for the Source of thought, you find (again, "it is seen") that there is nothing. No Thing. Abide in that, not knowing, not accepting any answer to the inquiry... all answers are mind trying to keep what it thinks is control (a huge illusion, that!)

There is NO controller actually, is there? Look for it. All you find is... nothing. The Self. And then the aha! Arises... that was never really missing! That, I Am.

The mind is NOT the "cause of suffering." There is nothing wrong with thoughts arising... like clouds in an empty sky, they come to pass, not to stay! The mind gives trouble ONLY when there is an un-rooted-up belief (acceptance of a thing as true despite there being no evidence for its actuality) in a separate 'person' called me who owns everything as a pseudo-subject (I think therefore I am – a real crap idea!) So, get to the cause... the belief in "me"... and no effects can remain. Then all manner of thoughts can still arise (out of the conditioned mind's habitual patterning) but when those thoughts are no longer believed to be "my" thoughts it's all over, and aliveness... Presence Awareness... is unconcealed once and for good. Then you ARE the Natural Stateless State of Being... just That. And it is seen that you were never actually anything BUT That.

Start from the simple knowingness, you already ARE what you seek. Keep that in awareness and that will assist in the investigation. Then as the whole house of cards falls in on itself and disappears, there can be a mighty laugh. "It was never NOT!"

As Nisargadatta said, "There must be earnestness." Keep at it... and stay in touch. Let's get all questions and doubts out and dissolved. Then all there is, is You, as That, Impersonal Awareness, I Am. Your True-Nature.

Keep going!

46. Scriptures Are Dead Words

Before I could reply, Paul added, *A question that keeps popping up in my mind is, why don't the scriptures or even the ancients just refer to God as just 'simple Presence Awareness or Being' instead of God?*

One of the reasons that I think scriptures trip people up is that it is projected as a me and God, or something outside of the self. Why couldn't they allude to THIS as just Awareness or Presence the way you, Tony, Gilbert, or Non-dual 'so-called people'?

It's a very good question. Now, who is asking?

That is just they way that cookie crumbled! All scriptures are dead words that attempt to represent the original speaker's message... but the representations are done, usually, many years after the organism through whom the message arose expired. But SOME "Ancients" did express this.

If you look at the essence of all the great traditions the seeds of this CAN be found: Buddha: Actions happen, deeds are done, but there is NO 'individual doer' thereof."

Paraphrasing Lao Tzu: "Everything happens, then the people say 'we did it'." And, "The Tao that can be spoken is NOT the Eternal Tao."

In the Bible, "I Am That I Am." Just that and nothing else. Then what gets dualized, so to speak, by the energy of dividing called 'mind,' is as you say, the dichotomy of "I" and "Thou."

Christ, in my seeing of it, said, "*I Am* is the Way, the Truth, the Life." Not the personal thought-form and body called "me, Jesus." The NON-conceptual I Am that is the a priori actuality, the absolute Presence Awareness.

Christian tradition: "Be still. And Know. I Am. God."

And, from the Hindu tradition: "Tat Tvam Asi - THAT Thou Art.". You Are That. All is Nothing but That.

No Thing/Every Thing. As in Zen.

> "In my hut this spring, there is nothing. There is everything."
>
> —Anonymous Zen master

In any case, ALL "why" questions tend to be a precursor to a story, more concepts for a believing entity to accept or reject. The functioning of the cosmic game of hide and seek! Rather than ask why, try on asking "Who asks why?"... who is that?

When the mind chatters, You (Presence Awareness appearing as Consciousness) might inquire "Who ARE You?" And you might notice, the so-called mind (which is only another pattern of Energy appearing as noise seemingly in "your head") that "it" scurries out of awareness, like a cockroach in the kitchen late at night scurries away when you switch on the light.

The phantom mind simply cannot survive the Light of your own Presence Awareness!

47. Dig In and Root Out the Source of All Fears

Gina writes, "I was first introduced to A Course in Miracles, and a very good friend of mine gave as a gift I Am That approximately 15 years ago. I love the book."

Here are a couple of great pointers from that work: "You ARE the Light of the world." That IS your True Being...and, paraphrasing, the Real can never be threatened; the unreal does not actually exist. Therein lies The Endless Fathomless Peace that you actually are.

A few months back a good friend of mine gave me a copy of "Sailor" Bob Adamson's book. I loved it but on finding your little book on the Internet it is made so much clearer. The past four years I have spent, doing nothing. At times very peaceful other times being upset at the fact that I don't get it. I get very tense, and feel like a zombie in limbo. So I am seeking still. That's why I loved your pointers. Thank you for sharing.

You are most welcome, dear One. WHO or WHAT feels or thinks? Who is "upset?" Who thinks 'they' are "doing nothing?" That's a belief in "someone" doing nothing. Look within, without effort. This is not a mediation practice! Now, paradoxically, it will seem to the phantom entity that IT is choosing to inquire. In actual fact, thoughts arise; some seem to be decisions or choices, some seem to be choices or other apparently volitional "free will" activities.

In Reality there is no chooser, no choice, no one to exert free will. Find the false nature of that "entity" through investigation and it's all over... and in fact it is then seen that it was all a dream. But until that is realized, keep at it. Again, a paradox.

No one else can give the seeing to you; the looking has to happen. Looking into the space of awareness, not as a practice but as a natural observing what is there, reveals it all. The questions, "Who Am I?" and "Who Is Asking?" are just prompts to be dropped after a few thoughts and then a looking into the space naturally occurs and you see (it is seen) that there is NO actual person in the organism. Even the idea "I am a body" is false, and insubstantial, like a cloud.

Forcing meditation is one way to avoid awakening, by the way! Who meditates? Let's discuss this! I also encourage you to re-read the book at bedtime, and if you fall asleep see who wakes up to finish it in the morning.

Give me a call and let's nail it down and end the dream of the false person seemingly suffering. I LOVE sharing the Good News. And if someone accuses a person of being half cooked, just see through that... it is a crap concept. WHO needs "cooking?" You ARE "THAT" which is sought. Anyone who tells you otherwise is likely just trying to gather a group of disciples... and that is total dualism at its most insidious, so far as it is seen here!

Sharing This is all I do! It is a joy and an honor, so to say! Dig in and get to the root of the panic... it is just the little phantom "me" that's afraid it will die... which it WILL but it does not necessarily have to be all that dramatic!

48. There Is Aaaahhhh

Follow-up from Gina:

Reading your message there is aahhhh thank you!... If something comes up I will call you.

Bless you Charlie.

And you, dear One.
Sounds good!
Love,
I Am

<u>Follow-up</u>

Allee Allee In Free

Gina calls. A question arises: *Why doesn't the "tiger" bite off my head and end this seeking?*

A response bubbles up "Out of Nowhere"... (Now, Here)... "well, Gina, any 'why' question simply leads to more story. What is needed is to find out if the story-TELLER is actually REAL. Or Not."

Then the next expression comes out: "A better question would be to ask, 'Who is asking why?'"

There is a moment of absolute silence, then she burst into the most joyous laughter I have ever heard. After a while she said, with a huge smile in her voice, "That blew 'me.'" Giggling still, she added "That's IT."

Welcome Back to your True Home, Gina. Love to you! That is, Love IS you... so love to love from love!

49. Nothing and Everything

Q: In your book you say that paradox and confusion are pointed to as the guardians at the gateless gate of seeing who you really are! Mind says one is right and the other is wrong. That is duality. A paradox is DISSOLVED (not resolved) in the Light of Not Knowing.

Bingo... !!

So I must agree that our true nature is "No Thing" (Just this and nothing else).

Drop the "I must agree." The "I" is the mind! Dropping that, the expression might be, "There is the seeing, that true nature is 'No Thing' (Just this and nothing else.)" The tweak also gets the "our" out of the way, leaving... No Thing. Nothingness appearing as everything. To paraphrase Nisargadatta Maharaj, when there is the seeing, by no one, that there is nothingness, that is wisdom. When there is the seeing, by no one, that there is everything, that is Love. And life flows between these two, as these two, which are not actually separate. The Absolute... Not Two!

So, you cannot get this with the mind. It is beyond the mind. But you use the mind to know the mind to get beyond the mind. Great paradox. Also notice that there is nothing noticing the noticer. That No Thing is what you are. Paradox again...

The paradox begins to dissolve in the clear seeing that "IT *is beyond the mind,* AND *you use the mind to know the mind to get beyond the mind.*" These "seeming two" are actually... Not Two. "Mind" is also IT, expressing (arising) in IT and AS an aspect of IT.

When the word "but" in your sentences is changed to AND, that begins to dissolve a paradox.

When But (dualism) is seen as more accurately as And (non-dual), right (t)here clarity begins. AND, clarity is also not "IT"... what "IT" is, is simply, Presence Awareness. "That" (as in I

Am That, or That Thou Art) is the indescribable Absolute Freedom. Period.

No one knows That. There is, as "you" are seeing now, NO one, no "individual." All there is, is the un-DIVIDED One-Essence. All there is, IS that. Appearing as not that and that.

Glad to be home again after years and years of suffering by a someone who turned out to be nobody.

Nobody, No One, Just This! Self-Knowing Presence Awareness, unknowable by a false "me." In Not Knowing, IT is seen that This alone (All One) Is Real!

It is all good for a mighty laugh, isn't it? Welcome back to the Home you never left!

Being. Just That.

50. The Final Seeing... And There "It" is

Causeless joy, the natural state of man!

Follow-up:

I just got an insight that I would like to share. Now that the search by nobody is over it is important to mention that the I (entity) may claim ownership of this seeing. If the phantom self (ego) does this, then the game of life will continue to suffer. This is the ego coming through the back door, so to speak, to claim ownership of this, so-called, new found seeing.

The claim is simply another thought arising in the invincible and untouched essence... Isness... that is both the "insight" and the noticing of it. If there is TRULY no sense of a self-center, that "claiming mechanism" is simply seen as another pattern of thought energy arising from and disappearing back into the empty sky-like Being... Awareness-Presence arising as Intelligence-Energy. It is then seen that an insubstantial truly non-existent "thing" cannot fixate and become a "real thing" that is "important."

Yesterday's insight can easily become today's new "enlightened ego" trip. While you are spot on with the insight, so long as it remains an *insight only* there will still be a VERY subtle sense that there is a someone to have the insight. Insights ultimately are no more significant than any other thought.

Here is a pointer from "Sailor Bob" Adamson:

> *Truth or Reality cannot be stored, cannot be amassed – it does not accumulate. The value of any insight, understanding, or realization can only be in the ever-fresh presence of the moment. Yesterday's realization is not a bit of good. Now it is dead. Now it has lost its vitality. It is useless to try and cling to or hold onto an insight, an understanding, or a realization, for only in its movement can there be the enabling of ever-fresh and new insights of Truth or Reality to appear. The idea of enlightenment or self-realization as a one-*

time event or a lasting and permanent state or experience is an erroneous concept.

Understand-ING or know-ING is alive in the immediacy which can never be negated. The emphasis is on the activity of know-ING which is going on as the immediacy now – not the dead concept "I understand" or "I know."

Watch the mind attempt to reassert its primacy over Presence Awareness! One way it does this is by thinking and writing such things as "It is important to mention." For whom is it "important?" Consider the possibility that NOTHING is ANY more important than anything else, in the appearance.

This is the (false but seeming real) entity-ego coming through the back door (*so to speak*) to claim ownership of this, so-called, new found seeing. The seeing is seen by no one. In reality, no separate person exists, so how can it claim ownership?

To summarize, suffering will soon follow if ownership is claimed by this entity called me-myself-I...

Along the pathless path this is a marvelous pointer. But again, that is just another opinion! As you are aware ALL pointers must eventually be discarded, not held as an affirming or asserting by the thought-up self-center. Be careful not to turn these pointers into assertions!

Here is a quote that helped me quite a lot, from the Hsin Hsin Ming of Seng T'san:

> *If you wish to see the truth then hold no opinions for or against anything. To set up what you like against what you dislike is the disease of the mind.*

Thank you for writing. This will benefit others. Just keep the sharing alive and real, holding onto nothing, fixating on nothing. Continue the inquiry... Who am I? Who? To whom did that "insight" occur!? Keep asking until there is no thinker left to ask... Who AM I?

51. Thanks for Setting Nobody on Fire

Nelson says, *Less than two months ago while vacationing with my wife, Jamie, there was the falling away of "me." I had been reading Bob's book* <u>What's Wrong with Right Now?: Unless You Think About It</u> *and then later as I was walking along the beach (How to say it?!) poof! There has been a period of stabilizing in What IS since then.*

Great news!! And as it is seen by no one (clear in your further expressions) there is no "stabilizing"... that is just another thought story arising presently. That Awareness-Presence IS and requires NO stabilizing, maintenance or deepening... those ideas are simply the habitual patterns of thought that seem to always make the case for "becoming." There is, as you see now, NO becoming possible as there is in fact already always no person and no where to go. This Is It.

There is a marvelous old Zen story: A novice asked the Master as they were just sitting, "Master, what happens next?" The old man replied, "Nothing happens next. This Is It."

Nothing <u>HAPPENS</u>... IT is No Thing... Happen-ING.

So all that is happening is Nothing... Happening!

Presence Awareness, The Absolute No Thing-ness, patterning as all the appearances AND non-appearances... nothing AND everything. Nothing is outside of everything (read that twice and see what you see!) And these are Not Two. Grok the paradox in that and it dissolves at once and no one sees.

Happy Un Birthday, dear Friend.

At any rate, my reason for writing you, Charlie, is that damn it if somehow after finding your book on-line a few days ago, the no one and nothing that I am just can't stop writing. I haven't even been able to get much passed Chapter One of your book because there is so much pouring out. I thought I'd share (since it's sort of your fault) and would love to get your feedback.

Thanks... and, as I know it is seen there (here), Charlie didn't do anything. By the way, when the idea of "credit" falls into the abyss and is seen no more, then blame goes with it. Ain't that SWEET!?

Below are some excerpts from my in-progress work (begun just two days ago!) tentatively entitled "I" am a corpse (& so are "you").

There is SO much great expression! I have selected a few to offer the feedback that just bubbles up to say:

...it is especially unfortunate how many so-called teachers of truth there are who not only tolerate the notion that there is some attainable thing called enlightenment but also actively perpetuate it. This is just plain wrong. Why? Because it would take someone (i.e., a self) to attain something called enlightenment and there is not a single self in existence.

I must say your writing is amazingly, lucid, clear, and clean. Your expression is so obviously coming straight out of No Thing (Self)... it resonates deeply... as it keeps coming out of the spaceless Space through a corpse named "(reader)", many who still believe they are separate from The Self will (seemingly) be led back to the Home they never left, as has happened for The former seeker!

One suggestion comes up to be shared: Try to stay clear of this or that being "wrong." All IS, as it is... including so called "False Prophets"...

You are making a great point here about the folly of the seeker-guru game. And, I encourage you to re-read and maybe add or alter the expression from your very big heart to say something along the lines of "Paradoxically, even these so-called teachers are The Absolute expressing AS the ignorance and all the purveyors of dualistic crap, and the believers that seem to themselves to be real, owing to a lack of actual investigation. Not Two!

You added a poem:

You are not a self.
A self is a lie.

You are the Sole Existent

which is the Eternal Self
without shape, duration or boundary.

Brilliantly clear and evocative! Nice pointer... "a self" is a lie... THE Self is Real. It might read just as well as "*a person*" *or a "me" is a lie*... your call.

People don't wake up.
Only the Self
is present awake-ness.
Sometimes the Self
in the guise of an apparent person
might appear to wake up.
But waking up is
not possible for the Self
which ever IS.

A great sort of Bottom Line! Only suggestion, drop the word "but." See how it feels then... Leave the reader to look at what's pointed to. The "But" NEGATES what went before. Dropping leaves a pointing as the paradox of *appear to wake up. Waking up is impossible.* That stresses the waking up as ONLY an appearance in This That Is.

The person having the experience that is sometimes labeled enlightenment (and is actually not an experience at all) would know they are not a person and that enlightenment simply and solely is. In short there is no one to be enlightened. Enlightenment just is! Enlightenment is the Self and the Self has no relation at all to the concept of a self.

"Enlightenment" is so overdone and misused a word that it tends to be listened to as some unattainable "state" that only "Masters" "attain."

I have pretty much stopped using words like "awakening, Enlightenment, Liberation..." in the perspective "here" (the non-perspective of no thing.) These bits of language tend to reinforce a belief that there is something to get... some day!

Presence Awareness always IS. That points out the never missing, only overlooked, "Is-Ness." Try changing that in the paragraph above and notice how it then occurs for Consciousness arising from Presence Awareness over there.

There is an ancient saying from India: "There is nothing that is not Shiva." Yes! There is No Thing, and THAT No Thing is NOT Shiva. Shiva is Consciousness arising from the Pure No Thing. It is a lovely... guess what? Paradox!

I look forward to seeing more as the Self expresses through the dead man talking over there. Thanks for writing!

52. No One Called Nobody

Nelson follows up: *Damned it if the words coming off of your fingertips and from my inbox and into these eyes aren't just the shining of This. No thing to no thing. It's like you say, Charlie, no thing is a happen-ing. It is in fact only this happen-ing that is happening.*

And that's That.

Such wonderful feedback! Especially regarding conceptual frameworks (which certainly don't fit with This) and worshiping dead Jnanis and hoisting good people (who are the same One all are) up onto pedestals. Who is there to do this sort of thing? No one ever of course.

Exactly.

Not much to add to this! The cake called "you" is clearly Baked, Iced, and Now, EATEN by Nothing. Just... NOW.

53. Viewpoint Of No Thing

Q: I just realized that the phantom self is really the one that is saying "the ego will slip through the back door." This is seen clearly from the viewpoint of "no thing" instead of from the viewpoint of "something."

And even this "viewpoint" of "nothing" is <u>also</u> seen as an object appearing in the mirror of Pure Presence, isn't it?

The mirror reflects but is itself untouched. Conceptually, you are the mirror, not the reflection or the thing reflected... no "viewpoint" actually exists in The Absolute.

Language simply cannot ever express It.

54. Love Is Yes in Silent Stillness That IS

So there's no one to thank. True You already Understands.

That is a dualistic concept and as such may lead to some confusion in the seeking mind.

"True You" understands absolutely nothing!

True You, non-dual "a priori" Awareness, is the <u>Is-ness</u> prior to understanding.

THAT is the silent seeing, knowing... and can never understand because it IS all.

The eye cannot see itself seeing. The brain cannot see itself thinking. The mind can seemingly understand itself. They call that philosophy and psychology, etc. This is all utterly irrelevant to That which cannot know the knower!

Non-conceptual Knowingness, or Awareness Presence, IS "izzing." The knower of all that is a false appearance and yet... these are not two!

Chew on that!

55. Aren't Doubts a 'Cognitive Hesitation' or Gap?

A friend wrote: *"I continue to be frustrated. Evidently the suffering continues and I cannot be sure why. I don't think I have 'doubts' as this word implies a cognitive hesitation or gap."*

Cognitive hesitation or gap? That is NOT what is being pointed to. Don't get stuck on a fancy concept. "Doubt" in this context is a pointing out that there is still a belief in a separate entity and a non-recognition of your own undeniable pure non-conceptual awareness. Consider what the free online dictionary at www.m-w.com says: "Doubt is to lack confidence in; to distrust." Let's Keep it SIMPLE and real!

Another "teacher" often uses this word and I think it is inappropriate in my case but perhaps I have doubts and don't recognize them. But is this possible? Aren't "doubts" always explicit?

NO. That is the whole problem! The digging with the inquiry reveals those subtle, thoroughly HIDDEN doubts, in the deep back story of "you." The mind... "you"... (NOT the Real Self that you are)... cannot know that these doubts exist until you get real with the pointers and go after them with earnestness.

The unexamined "I Thought" has grown innumerable branches upon branches since you first began believing "I am separate" at around the age of two or three. Now "you" are attempting to grasp That — Non-Conceptual Presence Awareness — with the mind. This Space of Knowing is No Thing that can ever be contained by the mind, which is itself a thing, and a thing can never see or know NO thing.

> *Before you can say "I am", you must be there to say it. Being need not be self-conscious. You need not know to be, but you must be to know.*
> —Sri Nisargadatta Maharaj

Do you exist? Are you not right there right now wherever you are? Try to escape Being. You CAN'T!

Isn't there the natural undeniable knowing, "I Am?" That is it... the big IT. Just That. You are, nothing but this "I Am." FULL STOP!!!

THIS that you ARE is beyond description. Get out of the mind. There is no light there!

Look deeply into this:

> *There is a principle which is a bar against all information, which is proof against all arguments and which cannot fail to keep a man in everlasting ignorance – that principle is contempt prior to investigation.*
>
> —Herbert Spencer

One thing that stands out for me reading your post is, "despite (various meetings)"... "I" continue to inquire and ponder. Turn back from there and look to see who inquires? Who ponders?

Who is frustrated? Who is suffering? Who is thinking, "I don't have doubts?" ALL that is going on is a repetitive pattern of mentation believed to be "I" that does all that.

You have had the injection. It will take the limited "you" out of the picture at its own pace, so long as there remains a belief in that "I" and a belief in "time."

The Energy-Intelligence aspect of Presence Awareness will keep you looking. It is unavoidable.

As the sage Ramana Maharshi put it, "Take comfort in the fact that your head is in the tiger's mouth." And stay in touch as spirit moves.

56. After Nothing Happens, Effortless Living Unfolds

But for no one.

Q: After seeing the false as false can suffering still arise?

Depends on what you mean by suffering. I define suffering as a thought or series of thoughts about what is present, like (all from my own experiences, not theoretical or hearsay)... "Something is wrong with ME," "my life is not what I want it to be," "Something is missing for me," "I wish I was a better person," "I don't want what I have", "I want what I don't have" and so on. Look and see if there are not thoughts like this arising where you are.

And then the add-ons to those happen, inventing a "past" now: "I should not have done that... I feel so guilty." "I should not have taken that route home. Then the car accident would not have happened." "If only I had not argued with my boss I would still have that great high paying job."

And more add-ons happen, inventing a "future" now: "If I don't find a source of income pretty quick I am gonna end up broke, homeless and die miserably on the street." "I have nobody to take care of me when I get too old to function." And the biggie, "Someday I am going to die. How awful. I hate my future but I want to live."

Rocks and hard places.

All that stuff creates resignation, deep sadness and despair, feeling inadequate, even powerlessness, hopelessness, deep depression, wild mood swings, violence to self and others, and a lot more psychologically based suffering... all of which arises a split-nanosecond AFTER the thinking arises. Why?

Have you noticed the one common ground for all these suffering ideas?

The "I" or "ME" thought.

When a thought "I" is taken to be the "Real I" the trouble begins and escalates so long as that core belief remains in place and unexamined. It can (I can report from personal experience) lead to a complete crash and what is usually termed a "nervous breakdown," (as happened to the Charlie-organism in 1974.)

Investigate – inquire into the "I" or me, asking "Who Am I?" What is a "me" and where do I find one in the space of my own always present conscious beingness? Doing the homework is the ONLY thing that finally worked to end <u>psychological</u> suffering for me.

And yet when the true Self... Awareness... is seen as true and the false (the phantom "entity") is seen as false... "suffering" can certainly appear... as an emotional pain like "sadness" or a thought "I am so tired" or "How will I find a new source of income to avoid a nasty old age?"... but the key word here is "appear." And when there is no BELIEF that the "I" or "me" is REAL, there is no psychological suffering... all that the psychological suffering is, is an overlay "on" <u>What Is</u>. So pain, or suffering if you like, HAPPENS... to no "person."

To paraphrase The Buddha, "There is suffering, but no one to suffer."

And that is freedom. Natural and unshakable no matter what arises. The screen is untouched by the movie.

57. Spiritual Suffering or Chemical Imbalance?

It occurs to me that something Stephen Wingate warned me about many moons ago could be an essential reminder to those still suffering (and perhaps it has gotten so severe that the mind is plagued with suicidal thought). It could be very useful to repeat here:

> *The concepts of non-duality that I share here will not heal broken bones, nor will they cure bi-polar disorder or acute depression. If you are experiencing acute psychological symptoms, please see a Doctor.*
>
> [Thanks to Stephen for his permission to quote this.]

Having suffered from BOTH bi-polar disorder and acute depression for about 60 years I second the motion... and urge any reader experiences these symptoms to GET PROFESSIONAL HELP.

Ultimately, once the clear seeing unfolds, the medications MAY be "weaned" (but ONLY under a doctor's supervision.) That happened for "me" back in July and I am grateful. But so long as symptoms persist, "knowing" they are "only a dream character's delusion" is a damn dangerous belief! Again, I speak from my own direct experience of this.

"Who Am I?" Ask till there is no one to ask. Then you might wonder, "Who is asking who I am?" And a mental impulse may arise, "I Am." Right here it essential not to take that thought as "the answer!" That "I am" is only another thought.

Give it back to inquiry: "Who said I Am? Who Am I In Reality?" Not as yet another thought looping back and forth – "Who Am I? I Am" – ad infinitum. That is not what is being pointed to. As I have said many times here and on my web site and other books, what is being pointed out is NON-conceptual, Self-Effulgent, Awareness-Presence, Always Fresh, Always expressing as Pure Consciousness right here, right now.

That is, ultimately, NOT the "Thought" I Am. It is Silence, Stillness, the underpinning, so to speak, of all thoughts, feelings, and every other object that appears. THAT is Non-Dual. Oneness. Being. No Thing.

And that is what you are.

Is that TRUE? See for yourself... do the homework and the cage of the conceptual prison will crumble into nothing... No Thing.

And see a doctor if you want to suicide, THEN come back to this pointing. There are no cures here... because, nothing is wrong in What You Are: Pure Presence arising as Consciousness and appearing as all that is.

58. When Did the Penny Drop?

An anonymous questioner asks: *When did "the penny drop" (so to speak) for you, Charlie?*

Three answers:

Answer One: About a hundred and ninety times, over thirty years, in the last three years often followed by a global e-mail and made global phone calls, announcing to all and sundry, *I GOT IT.* The freakin' penny finally dropped. I am Enlightened! Hot DAMN!

Can you smell the "person infected with Mania?" The "Transformed Ego-Mind" is a weird and convoluted, twisted and fascinating thing for "another mind" to behold. And yet that too is Divine... so to say...

The Real Friends wrote back in response to that assertion of some "attainment" by "me" and said, "Who got WHAT!? It's BULLSHIT. There is NOTHING TO GET!"

Answer Two: In early July 2006.

Answer Three: *Never.* (Truly speaking.)

Ultimately: What penny? There never WAS a penny or any dropping thereof. Nor was there ever a separate entity for which dropping happened. No dropping and no Charlie. It all was just a show. The show goes on but no "person" is left to take it personally or seriously.

As the non-dual Buddhists like to chant... Gate Gate Paragate Parasamagate. (gone, gone, gone beyond!)

Bodhi Svaha! (Hooray!)

Now: This is totally beyond the grasp of thought. Don't try to figure it out. Just look: Who Am I? I know I am. That is undeniable. Who is the "I" pointed to in the THOUGHT "I Am?" Find out.

Thanks for a good question!

59. Mommy, There's Something I Don't Understand.

A precocious little girl asks:

What's an I, Mommy?

What do you mean, little one?

You say I about you all the time. And you tell me, "if you want something say 'May I have it please?' Then I is me and I is you? What do you mean by I? And what's a you? If I say you and you say I. which one is I and which one is you?"

Ask your father!

60. If I Let Go and JUST BE, Won't I Go Bankrupt?

Q: I am worried about this message that there is no one and nothing I can do. If I just give up all my commitments and forget about getting a new job or somehow finding the money to pay my bills and credit cards off won't I just end up bankrupt? I don't want that! How does the non-dual message help with this? Please help! I am real worried about this! It's making me sick. I am so afraid of being broke!

Dear friend: I know that emotional story quite well! I have had many of the same concerns and for most of my life have always been worried sick about how I would make ends meet. What the non-dual teachings point to is, that in actual fact, this stuff is all an *imagined future*, a story arising here and now, that is in play, and this is seemingly causing suffering. For WHOM, is the question.

There is no way to know whether bankruptcy will happen or not. You may work very hard and still go bankrupt. That happened to me in 1974! Stuff happened like lease companies going bankrupt plus gasoline shortages that stopped my Ferrari business dead in its tracks!

Besides that, right here and now in the Charlie-story, savings are dwindling, bills are mounting, worries arise about how the rent will be paid... and shit yeah, it seems really REAL!

So what?
I had no control.
I have no control.
Never did!
Not then. Nor do I have any control now.
Neither does anyone else.

But ALL that is the story of an "I." Is it ACTUALLY real?

What IS real and invincible? What is the only True Reality? Self, Presence Awareness, Being... just That. And what appears as a story in the life of an apparent individual is ALSO that. This is the grand paradox of NON-duality.

The question you are asking, "if there is no one, what can I do?" is based on the core false premise, an assumption, that there is a "I" who must do something to make sure "I" don't go bankrupt and lose everything. There is no such. And yet the appearance of this "separate desperate 'I'" is also Being, appearing as NOT Being! Paradox on top of Paradox!

In regards to helping, this message does not actually offer any "help." It's more for looking within to see, who is this "I" that thinks "I need help?" And looking within AND NOT looking within are also Being, appearing as THAT TOO.

These Paradoxes are Being, Paradoxing.

(A side note: There are lots of places that offer practical help in the life-dream story, for financial issues; government and state agencies, credit counseling firms and the like. Ask your banker or look in the white pages under government. Welfare, job assistance, food stamps etc... all sorts of resources are available. And, Being is appearing presently as a "person" availing or not availing itself of those resources. There is no controller. The one who thinks it controls is Being arising presently as a believing that It is a separate controlling entity. Yes, that too is not two.)

The message of Non-duality is, in essence, that there is no you (as you noted) AND so long as there is a story of a "me" who is the "owner" of "my life" being taken as REAL, investigation into what or who thinks that stuff might well be undertaken. Then perhaps the story will be seen AS a story arising presently, and when that's the case, what bother can it be? It is only a bother to an identified "entity" that is in fact only the "I" thought, with many added thoughts all taken to be "Who I Am." And all it is, is a story. A never-ending tale of pain and pleasure!

That is where I found the inquiry (Who Am I? Who is worried or afraid?) to be of "interim" value, for so-called people, *in the story*. Ultimately, the Teachings of Nisargadatta and the sages of old are about taking the (apparent) individual beyond the NEED for any help. However so long as a "me" is believed to be real, the pointers are there to assist. This is a paradox. There is no person, AND so long as there SEEMS to be a person, the "person" can be led to inquire within! "Who Am I?"

This all happens of its own accord. It dawns on the "individual" that what that individual is, is a phantom of its own opera. With much agony and a little ecstasy! Seen a good Opera lately? Then you know what I mean. Why are "soap operas" so popular?

Until this is all seen to be a movie-story and NOT what you are, you are the star in your own movie-story. And so long as there is a belief in a "me" that IS REAL and has to manage its life, life will be a roller-coaster ride. You are not driving your life any more than a rider on the coaster drives the coaster. As the story is seen to be unreal, life may still be a roller-coaster ride, but with no bother to the rider.

Take a look at this pointer: Were you worried about getting enough to eat or finding a job, when you were in your mother's womb? Have you considered this?

This entire story is arising where you are (here.) Without Awareness, Being, it cannot arise at all. So perhaps you will see now that, without Being, Consciousness Itself, not a thing actually is. All there is, is Source, Awareness, Consciousness. Not the label; the actual.

What is the Source of Source?

All this is Being. Being, being thoughts and fears. Being, being worried about an imaginary future. Being, being scared or sad, or happy and peaceful.

What you are, is This: Being-All-That-Is. Nothing is left out. All is being. And that appears in the dream character's dream story as "worried about money."

There is nothing to fix. There is no one to fix it. Relax if you can. Let the One who nurtured the body-mind you consider to be "you" in the womb take care of matters. You are NOT in charge here!

If there were anyone there I would tell that anyone to... Let go. Just Be. Easy enough, since you already ARE Be-ing. Being Everything, as it is. There is Nothing and no one left out of What You Are. Being, being afraid. Being, being sick. Being, being worried. Being, being depressed. Being, being happy. Etc.

All IS Being. Nothing but That.

61. Ask Yourself Who Am I? Until You Drop!

Q: I have been enjoying the rough draft copy of the manuscript, "From I Am To I Am With Love," that you sent me and have listened to your Meeting CD several times! Clarity with Laughs - why, of course :)

Glad it's resonating!

Things are settling in "beyond my control" as spontaneous insights "pop up out of the blue" as I go about my daily routine. Having tasted the Truth in moments of clarity, there seems to be no turning back... regardless of the apparent psychological suffering which still seems to persist.

All that allows it to persist is that the investigation into the "me" that seems to suffer has yet to be taken up in real earnestness. Asking WHO suffers, WHO is this "me" that believes it is real – "WHO AM I?" As Ramana Maharshi pointed out, the thought "Who Am I?" will destroy all other thoughts, and will itself be burnt up in the end, like the stick used to stir the burning pyre is itself destroyed.

Ask yourself "Who Am I?" Ask until "you" drop!

Situations seemed to pull "me" back into old habitual patterns of thought and feeling where all interest in self-enquiry and non-duality were replaced with "worldly" matters of control and worry. You know the "story" :) And yet, this inner pull towards the Light cannot be denied.

Correct. AND so long as there is suffering ask who is suffering. Whose habits? Whose thoughts? Whose feelings?

It sounds like you are right on the "Trackless Track." Just keep the investigation going into what you are not, via the Quest... "Who Am I?" Always seeing you are Already Always Presence Awareness, undeniable and invincible.

It's working for many, who find they are no longer seekers and no longer suffering. Might as well go for it 110 percent!

62. Are You Saying That There's No Free Will?

Q: This came up this morning as I was reading your web site: You are saying in effect, that we have no free will, right?

Actually "I" am saying nothing. All that there is here is an appearance of a thing typing. The pointers point. The One-Essence arises as letters and words and spaces and are then "read" by another appearance... that still perhaps has not seen that it is ONLY an appearance and <u>not an actual separate entity.</u>

That does not match up with my experience of being alive and holding down a job, choosing a new car, taking care of business and so on. If I have no free will, how is it that I can make decisions, select from a menu at lunch, and all the other decisions I make every day?

Decisions and choices arise along with an apparent chooser-decider. But isn't all that just thoughts? Who is the thinker? Look into this.

It seems to be a false assertion, like the philosophy of no-doer that is so prevalent in India, which you have to admit is a mess!

India a mess? Who says this is so? This idea is simply another thought story arising presently where "you" are... but you seem to turn stories into something that "Actually Is." That is the fundamental unseen error the unexamined thinker makes.

What is the evidence for this radical claim you make?

There is no evidence, simply because this is a pointer, meant to guide your own investigation, and NOT a claim, an assertion or a declaration. There is no "authority" for this outside of your own True Nature! There is no evidence outside of a story! Look into your own seeing, and conduct your own investigation, into what thinks, what decides, who chooses, etc.

Who is really in charge? Have you looked beyond the conviction of the separate "I" that in fact is just a thought form arising presently in the unbounded Awareness that you know as your own sense of being? Being is undeniable. All assertions of acceptance or denial simply arise as THOUGHT in that Space-Like Awareness of simple ordinary knowing. I exist. I am.

You cannot escape Being. That is a Self-Evident knowingness that requires absolutely no evidence. This pointing happening here is neither an assertion nor a declaration. Not a claim made by an "I." If the revered thinker-decider "I" is <u>"naught but a thought,"</u> then the saying, I assert and I decide and I choose, must be extensions of that Original Thought. And is the thought the actual? Try drinking the thought "water."

In the beginning is the Word, and the word is "I." ONLY a word. And a word is powerless to DO or NOT DO Anything.

What is, BEFORE the beginning? That is what needs to be uncovered. Then the whole story of this or that being right or wrong falls back into the Being out of which it bubbles up. Then there is No One Home and that Paradoxically is the REAL Home you Never Left.

What is the bottom line on all this?

All this is pointing to That which IS, yet cannot be expressed in concepts:

- You have no control or free will.
- How so? Simple. There is no "you.'
- You are a thought. Nothing more.
- How can a thought have any volition?
- If you believe these pointers, look and see who believes.
- If you do not believe these pointers, look and see who does not believe.
- You have no control.
- AND as long as "someone" thinks he or she exists as a separate entity and has control or no control...
- Put that "thinker" to work asking...
- Who Thinks, Believes, Knows or does not know....

63. Intellectual Understanding Is Not It

After a few e-mails and telephone consultations, Justin writes a follow-up: *It's so clear, that no "you" can "figure this out" – intellectual understanding ain't it!!*

Exactly.

Here is how the investigation went here: Through self-inquiry, the investigation (who am I, who sees, who hears, who thinks, who tastes, who is scared, who is anxious, who is any of this happening to...who am I?) revealed that there is no one/me "in the machine" living "my" life.

Bingo!

Since our dialogues began less than a year ago, it's amazing that now there's no suffering. That suffering that seemed to be so real. The "I" now seen moment by moment, to be totally false; there is no separate "me."

That's IT. Clear as a "dharma bell."

The "I" that I always thought I was, is only a thought, a false belief in a fictional reference point. The investigation truly uncovers this false belief (yet seeming to be VERY REAL) in me.

Beautifully stated.

My continuous story, which really sucked by the way: insecure, unhappy, angry, yada yada... In my particular search, it was absolutely paramount to have conversations with you as the reading of endless books, the listening to the same CDs over and over and over again, left me "half baked", confused and frustrated.

And yet, as you now know, there is no you or me... only the Presencing of that natural Awareness of Being. And <u>You</u> were always your own actual "teacher," not Charlie. Your own earnestness and willingness to toss all you believed you were into the fire of Inquiry is the key. Now you know Who You Are, AND who You are not!

Now you are done. Baked, Cooked, and Eaten by the "Tiger"... Your Very Own Self! Bodhi Svaha!

I've been able to tell you about ANYTHING in my story without apprehension and you have ALWAYS received me with loving honesty, openness and compassion. You continue to point the way home, as it is so easy to get lost along the way, so to speak.

That is why I feel such deep gratitude to "Sailor" Bob Adamson, John Wheeler, Annette and the others who are no longer suffering. They offered me that same open safe Space, to just BE and get all the stories of "me" out to be investigated. Just Now, they pointed it out to Charlie, just Now Charlie pointed it out to Justin, and just Now Justin may well point this endless peace out to others as well. Who knows? No one does.

Helping to point others to what can end their suffering is a life well worth living.

I have the deepest appreciation for meeting you in the dream. To those who haven't spoken to Charlie, call him; he'll point you home.

The appreciation goes to and thanks arise for the ancient, authentic lineage of Bob, Sri Nisargadatta, Siddharameshwar, and all the way back to the endless, beginningless beginning of "time." This is the lineage *of The Navnath Sampradaya...* It's the Real Deal. Bob once told me (I paraphrase, neither of us would remember the exact words!) that this entire ancient lineage (of true sages) is behind this. You cannot fail to "come home." And now you, Justin, are part of − and the whole of − this Sacred Lineage!

Justin offers a final reminder: *You (dear readers) are Already There (here.)*

And that is That. This is just beautiful, Justin... Happiness bubbles up here for (no) you! Thanks for writing. Stay in touch as Self moves to do so!

64. No Longer Any Case of Mistaken Identity

Edgar wrote, *Thank you again Charlie for your time and patience, the email and phone conversation has been very meaningful to me.*

You are very welcome.

I am taking your suggestion to heart and applying myself to the basics as best I can, seeing that I am this ordinary awareness and also looking and seeing that there is nothing there that the thought "I" applies to (no separate self to be found, only an assumed one).

Full stop!
All that "I" thought is, is a case of mistaken identity.

Having said that, I still feel that it would being very supportive if I continue to make John's talks when I can and if its all right I would like to speak with you on the phone from time to time.

That all sounds perfect. Give John a hug for me!

Follow-up

The best news ever:

Edgar Writes, *you note in your "Koan," "The source of Being is Not-Being. What is the Source of Not-Being?"*
My answer: The computer is screen is white.

Who answers? what screen? who knows?
No answer no question
de nada timeless wordless singularity
no words no not-words
in Love
Svaha!

The sound of traffic outside is registering in this singularity... I have heard this question another way, it goes something like this: The 10,000 things return to the one, what does the one return to?

> What one? There is no one
> not two not one
> what is?
> THIS....
> traffic sounds who hears?
> Sights - who sees?
> no one.
> clicking keys white spaces
> breathing whose?
> no one's
> full stop!

OK, sounds good... Thoughts aren't real, and everything I know about myself is a thought .. no self and therefore no person to know, realize or suffer, just this ordinary awareness still rooting out the "me" thoughts. All that is can be seen immediately. Nobody sees, just seeing.

That's a BINGO

Follow-up Two

There is just this awareness which thoughts and the world take place within, ideas of "me" come and go. The ideas are made of memory, hope and fear and no one can be found that they refer to. I am the witnessing awareness of all phenomena, it is no-thing and yet contains all.

Asking the Great question "Who Am I?", a multitude of answers and assumptions appear, but have no substance or independent nature of their own.

Yes, and ultimately (HERE NOW) all thoughts disappear, along with the thinker. The question "Who Am I?" burns everything to a crisp, including the question and the questioner! No more questioner, hence no more questions.

Even the *maha-question* "Who Am I?" is burnt out

The stuff of the mind I have taken as the self is made of a dream, and as all life changes within the awareness it also is this dream. No thinking or no belief in thinking means nothing to be sought and no seeker, no one to question or be confused. No self to be hurt or be diminished, no one dies and no one was born. Just this, this presence, this moment.

That is as well said as it gets! Welcome Home.

Coda to the Riff

> *You cannot negate that Knowing that You Are.*
> *It is not dead; it is not empty or silent stillness. Is not about*
> *keeping the mind silent, but seeing that what is prior to the*
> *'mind' is the very living-ness itself. It is very subtle... You are*
> *that!*
>
> —"Sailor" Bob Adamson

Looking for the Keys... Where They Aren't

Once upon a time there was a fellow who lost his house keys. He was frantically searching for them under the street light, in the overgrown brush, digging and perspiring. He had been at it for more than a half hour when a neighbor, out for a stroll, happened onto the scene.

"What are you searching for, my friend?", the neighbor inquired.

"My house keys! I can't get in my house and I am so tired and I have an early appointment! It is so frustrating!"

The kindly neighbor knelt down and said, "Here, I will help you look for them." After both dug around for a few minutes to no avail, the neighbor asked, "Do you recall, about where did you drop the keys?"

The hapless fellow replied, "Oh, I lost them over there by the door to the house. But you see, there is no LIGHT over there!"

We are like the seeker of the keys in that we seek the Peace of Being-Awareness where it isn't... in the MIND. There are no answers (or endless answers and endless questions if you prefer) in the "thinking machine" we call "the mind."

Looking in the apparent light for the Self that IS our True Nature is very much like looking for the keys where they are not just because there is some seeming light there.

But the light of the "mind" is actually darkness, compared to the brightly shining Light of the undeniable Presence Awareness IN and AS the thought-feeling-story ARISING.

The moral of the story is, Right NOW, Just stop looking for the Self where it isn't!

Two aspects of the "heart" are spoken of here: one is acceptable and the other is to be ignored. The heart that is part of this physical body and is located in one part of the body may be ignored! The heart which is acceptable is of the nature of pure consciousness. It is both inside and outside and it is neither inside nor outside. This is the principal heart and in it is reflected everything which is in the universe, and it is the treasure-house of all wealth. Consciousness alone is the heart of all beings, not the piece of flesh which people call the heart!

—Vasishtha's Yoga

PS: Who's in Charge?

I recommend that if there is any trace of suffering left in the space, that you browse through this book, starting with the undeniable fact of your Beingness which is expressed as the thought "I am, I exist, no doubt about it;" and then take on the *lovingly looking within* (not thinking about it!) until you are absolutely certain that there never was a separate entity with any control or volition.

As a certain book advises, consider that your looking needs to be along the lines of (to paraphrase) seeing the things you cannot change, changing what you can, and being graced by having the wisdom to see the difference. Then if you were to draw two columns on a sheet of paper, and list in the right hand column all the things you can't change and in the left hand column all the things you can change, then take your best shot at changing those that "you think" you can alter, modify, change, correct or improve in some fashion. Then, as you discover the always present failure to change a thing, move it to the right hand column. Then you will see that every single item has ended up in the right hand column!

Who Is Separate From All That Is?

If there is no separate "entity" in charge and able to change ANYTHING, it must be seen clearly that all attempts to do so are doomed to failure. Then what? You ARE. Just Being-Awareness, and there is no seeker left to suffer. All life continues as an appearance... but for no person... and ultimately, right here and now, it is seen that in Reality, all there is, is Being, and stories arising presently that are no longer believed to be real, but seen as a dream just like the dream story in sleep-dreams.

You've Been "Anti-Virused!"

Okay. You have had the injection. The anti-virus is on board. It will destroy the virus of the false belief in separateness... and then, as said many times here, there will be nothing happening to no one and everything appearing to no one.

All "being said" here in this "book" is various stories appearing presently. And all stories begin with "Once upon a time." See that the belief in the concept of time is only another arising and subsiding story appearing presently, and where is a problem with a story? It's entertaining, BUT... it never actually happened!

All "stories"... are energy arising from the Uncaused Source... Just Aliveness, patterning thoughts and an apparent thinker. All false and seen as such!

All is well.

Be well. You Are.

Be well. You Are.

Be as You Are.

Does Exist. Cannot Be Expressed.
—David Carse

Appendix One: Non-Duality Web Sites

"Sailor Bob" Adamson	http://members.iinet.net.au/~adamson7 http://www.sailorbob.net
John Wheeler	http://www.employees.org/~johnwhee
Annette Nibley	http://www.whatneverchanges.com
John Greven	http://www.onenessjustthat.com
Leo Hartong	http://www.awakeningtothedream.com
Burt Jurgens	http://www.beyonddescription.net
Gilbert Schultz	http://www.shiningthroughthemind.net
Stephen Wingate	http://livinginpeace-thenaturalstate.com
Mark West	http://gleaningsfromnisargadatta.net
Brian and Naama Lake	http://www.awarenessthatsimple.com
James Braha	http://www.jamesbraha.com/non_duality.html
Sri Nisargadatta Maharaj	http://www.nisargadatta.net
Nisargadatta Quotes	http://www.mpeters.de/nisargadatta/index.cfm

Appendix Two: Books for Browsing

I Am That, Talks with Sri Nisargadatta Maharaj, Acorn Press

What's Wrong with Right Now Unless You Think About It? and Presence-Awareness, Just This and Nothing Else, both by "Sailor" Bob Adamson

Awakening to The Natural State, Shining in Plain View, and Right Here, Right Now, all by John Wheeler

Oneness: The Destination You Never Left by John Greven

Beyond Description by Burt Jurgens
Available at www.beyonddescription.net

Be As You Are The teachings of Sri Ramana Maharshi, edited by David Godman

Perfect Brilliant Stillness by David Carse

Clarity, Already Awake and Being: The Bottom Line, all by Nathan Gill

Awakening To The Dream and Self to Self, both by Leo Hartong

Living Reality by James Braha

Everything is Clear and Obvious by Gilbert Schultz
Available at www.shiningthroughthemind.net

Consciousness and The Absolute and Prior to Consciousness, Talks with Sri Nisargadatta Maharaj, edited by Jean Dunn

Meetings

Abiding As Being - The Home You Never Left

Meetings happen on most Tuesdays and Thursdays from 7:30 till 9 PM and Sundays from 10 AM till 11:30 PM with refreshments afterward on Sundays. A $10 donation is suggested, but no one is ever turned away due to a lack of funds. *CALL or e-mail to confirm that there is a meeting on the day you wish to attend.* To RSVP, or to schedule a personal meeting or a telephone discussion with Charlie, contact by e-mail(charliehayes36@yahoo.com) or call USA +1 714 708 2311

The Pointless Point

"I know beyond doubt, that what I am IS Presence Awareness. So are you. We were never NOT That. I have not attained some awakening or liberation or some other mythical mystical 'state.' I have nothing you don't have. I'm NOT a teacher or a 'Guru.' These meetings are space for sharing what has worked for me, to finally relieve suffering once and for all, because I have an interest in helping others who are suffering find this natural peace."

Meetings are held at 1601 W MacArthur Blvd # 1-R
South Coast Metro (Santa Ana) CA 92704
Telephone 714-708-2311
e-mail: charliehayes36@yahoo.com

All are welcome.

For directions, call, or see the web page:
www.awake-now.org/directions.html

You are also invited to visit www.awake-now.org and submit questions and/or comments. See you there (Here.)

One on One

If you would like to engage in a direct consultation to re-solve doubts and questions, feel free to ask about that.

Charlie is retired, and so quite available. There is no set fee but donations are always welcome and much appreciated.

One on one consults often quickly dissolve all niggling vestiges of false belief and the never-absent True Nature is then no longer (seemingly) obscured.

Contact:

E-mail charliehayes36@yahoo.com or call USA + 1 714 708 2311 for details or to set up an appointment.

> WWhen I know I am nothing, that is wisdom. When I know I am everything, that is Love. And my life flows between these two.
>
> —Sri Nisargadatta Maharaj

Much Ado About Noth-ing

Welcome Home To Being —
The Abode You Never Really Left

www.awake-now.org